THIS BLESSED PLOT

by

HESKETH PEARSON

and

HUGH KINGSMILL

Illustrated by

MAURICE WEIGHTMAN

METHUEN & CO. LTD. LONDON
36 Essex Street, Strand, W.C.2

First published in 1942

PRINTED IN GREAT BRITAIN

THIS BLESSED PLOT

TO

ALAN WHITE

CONTENTS

THIS BLESSED PLOT

CONTENTS

A Proposal

One day in January 1939 Hesketh Pearson, who was feeling a little under the weather, told Hugh Kingsmill that he was going into the country for a few days, and asked Kingsmill if he could accompany him. Never

having seen Marlborough, he was going there first, and then to the Cotswolds.

It was a year and a half since they had gone round Scotland in the footsteps of Johnson and Boswell, and it now seemed to them that the moment had come to follow any Englishman whom they could pursue not too arduously in England, and who at the same time was sufficiently before the public to arouse the interest and stimulate the generosity of their publisher, Hamish Hamilton. After a brief discussion they arrived at the foregone conclusion that Shakespeare was their man, and hoping that he would be Hamish's too, they called at 90 Great Russell Street.

After they had outlined their plan, the following dialogue developed itself.

Hamilton: It's—it's very good of you two fellows to bring me this idea, but I'm afraid that at the moment people won't read anything but politics.

Kingsmill: And that's getting you down a bit?

Pearson: Hence our desire to lift you into a cleaner atmosphere.

Hamilton: Thanks. . . .

Kingsmill: But not so clean as to deprive you of all hope of profit.

Hamilton: Yes, but . . .

Pearson: Pull yourself together, Hamish, and listen carefully to me. Since Munich the English have begun to stir themselves. They are getting sick of being bawled at by all the Yahoos on the Continent. Shakespeare went through exactly what we are going through now—'Bragging horror' is what he calls it. And it was the spirit of Shakespeare that beat Spain, just as it will be the spirit of Shakespeare that will smash these Nordic Dagos.

Hamilton: Are you two proposing a patriotic pamphlet?

Pearson: Of course not. All we want is a short holiday in Shakespeare's country.

Kingsmill: Hesketh has never been to Marlborough, so that is to be our starting-place. We are just going to wander about that part of the world, drifting gradually towards Stratford, and piecing Shakespeare together as we go.

Hamilton: Piecing . . . Shakespeare . . . ? Together?

Kingsmill (*after a brief silence*): Well, Hamish, we mustn't take up your time. You've been very good to us in the past.

They rose, and Pearson, shaking Hamish's hand cordially, said he must lunch with them some day. Hamish said he would be delighted, and Pearson must give him a ring.

Pearson and Kingsmill walked thoughtfully to the Horseshoe in Tottenham Court Road, where they decided over a drink that there was nothing for it but to let Hamish go his own wild way.

The days went by. It was a wet dark month, and Pearson and Kingsmill came to the conclusion that the placing of the book might properly be shelved to a more clement season. Meanwhile, said Pearson, he must have his holiday, and would Kingsmill come with him as his guest?

A Sombre Start

On Monday, January 23, they left Paddington for Marlborough. The day was grey and rainy. Pearson and Kingsmill drooped opposite one another.

Pearson (*looking out of the window*): Poor old Shakespeare! How those factory chimneys would have got him down!

Kingsmill: How everything *did* get him down!

Pearson: Yes, his England wasn't a paradise either—the landscape dotted with gibbets, the festering corpses dangling in chains.

Kingsmill: Is it Bradley or Dowden who suggests that *Timon of Athens* is riddled with syphilis?

Pearson: Or is it Masefield?

Kingsmill: I was looking at *Timon* the other day, and what struck me was that when he gets to sex his universal vituperation rises to an almost inarticulate scream. There's one passage which is so incoherent that it can only be explained as a muttered imprecation on some personal memory. Timon is talking to the two prostitutes, and says:

'Be whores still;
And he whose pious breath seeks to convert you,
Be strong in whore, allure him, burn him up;
Let your close fire predominate his smoke,
And be no turncoats: yet may your pains, six months,
Be quite contrary: and thatch your poor thin roofs
With burdens of the dead; some that were hang'd,
No matter.'

I puzzled over this for a long time, and the meaning seems to be that the act of sex with these women instead of creating life in nine months breeds death in six. And then the picture after the thought—the tattered roof above the prostitute's room, thatched with the bodies of her clients. And that 'Some that were hang'd, no matter', which has absolutely no place in the play and can only refer to the fate of some one Shakespeare knew.

Pearson (pensively): The spacious days of great Elizabeth. . . .

From the train they could see the wooded slopes beyond the Thames.

Pearson: There's Goring, where Oscar Wilde used to . . .

Kingsmill: Used to what?

Pearson: Well, now you ask me, I really can't say. One knows he loathed nature in the raw, and anything out of doors was raw to Oscar, and one knows that when he was indoors he wasn't writing, because it was too much strain. Of course, there are stories about his private life, but my own opinion is that he never did anything at all, which explains my liking for him.

Kingsmill: It's sad to think that the next time he was on this line after his last visit to Goring was on his way to Reading Gaol, which I presume is in or near Reading.

Pearson: If you'll wait a minute or two, I'll show you the actual spot.

The train approached Reading, and Pearson, standing up, indicated a dull-bricked building with pseudo-Gothic turrets. 'There you are—Oscar's last country house.' 'Well,' mused Kingsmill, 'we're collecting material for our patriotic pamphlet.'

Pearson peered at the countryside through the rain-streaked windows. 'Whenever I am on this line,' he said, 'I remember that remark made by Sherlock Holmes to Watson on one of their crime jaunts to the west—something to the effect that those creeper-clad cottages, the praises of which, my dear Watson, you have just been singing, conceal crimes compared with which the agonies of women hammered by gin-sodden brutes in hideous alleys are an absolute picnic. Holmes was right. Leave little clumps of people to fester together, and everything they do and think is poisoned.' 'I quite agree,' said Kingsmill. 'The permutations and combinations in a nice old English village are matter for a higher mathematician. Every man his own mother, is the only way I can put it.'

Marlborough

As they left the station at Marlborough, and saw the pleasant red-brick town on the slope across the valley, their spirits rose. Passing the Bear and Castle, Kingsmill remembered that he had once put up at it on a visit with his father, so they turned in there. From a window on the second floor they looked out towards Savernake Forest, and saw a line of youths in shorts disappearing over the brow of the hill into the trees. Kingsmill sighed. 'So they still do it,' he murmured. 'I wish the sight of what Dean Farrar calls "young, eager life" didn't cool me so much. I suppose it's because of all the Victorian sentimentalization of public schools, of which I had so much at Harrow.'

Pearson: I liked running at school. It was the only thing into which the team spirit couldn't be introduced.

Kingsmill: You were also in your cricket eleven, weren't you? What always struck me about cricket was that it combined the most painful form of team spirit for those who weren't good

at it with the most liberal indulgence in exhibition-
ism for those who were.

Leaving the inn they walked out into the High Street,
Pearson, entranced with its spaciousness, exclaiming:
'It's as broad as most streets are long. One can really
fill one's lungs here.'

Kingsmill: We might go and look at the school,
which I haven't seen since my cousin was here.
That was in 1910, just before King Edward's death.
What a lot of nonsense is talked nowadays about

Edwardian times! I am always coming across
references by people of our age to the spacious
world in which their youth was passed, and of
course they wind up with Talleyrand's remark
that only those who had lived before the French
Revolution knew how good life could be—Talleyrand with the dew on him! Piping down the
valleys wild, piping songs of pleasant glee!
Personally I much prefer the present time to that
overfed stuffy age. I remember my brother
Arnold telling me how he went into a London
church at the end of 1914, just after the whole
population of **Antwerp** had been blown into the

Scheldt or blasted into the dykes. The preacher, a comfortable comatose gentleman, gave a little talk on the sufferings of the Early Christians, and then proceeded—'Living as we do in safer and more tranquil times . . .'

On entering the school yard they paused, and inquired from a boy of seventeen or so if they could see the school chapel. At once and very courteously he took them there, and asked if there was anything else he could do for them. After he had left them, they looked at each other in mild surprise, agreeing that here was further evidence of a change for the better in the present age. In their youth most boys would have greeted a query about the school chapel with a brutish grin.

Continuing their round they came to the newly-erected Science Building, and were a little dashed.

Kingsmill: Why put up buildings in which the art of blowing buildings to bits is studied?

Pearson: Science is the new Mumbo-Jumbo. One must admit that this sort of rot was only in its infancy in our time.

Cromwell at the Forge

Passing through what had once been the old Castle Inn, and was now a school house, they strolled down a gravel walk to a lawn beyond which, on the other side of a stream, rose a steep slope crowned by a line of trees. Soothed by this beautiful scene, they left the school grounds, and going along a lane came to some old buildings outside which a man was smoking. 'Seventeenth century?' Kingsmill inquired of Pearson. 'Early Tudor, at the very latest,' Pearson replied, and turned to the man for further information. 'They're old enough,' said the man. 'I live in 'em. But if you want something really historic, that's the old forge,' pointing across the road.

Kingsmill: Historic?

Man: Yes, the blacksmith there refused to shoe Cromwell's horse, so Cromwell tied him under his horse's belly, and took him back to London, where he put him in the Tower.

The travellers, thanking him, went over to the forge, and peered into the gloomy interior, where the blacksmith was hammering on an anvil. Asked to confirm the story about his seventeenth century predecessor, he replied curtly: 'That's how history grows.'

Two Interiors

In the evening they strolled down the High Street, looking for a comfortable pub. Passing a lighted window which suggested warmth and drinks within, they pressed their faces against the panes and took a preliminary survey. It was a pleasant lounge, well-lighted and well-filled. There were ten occupants. Three were asleep, six were not awake, and the tenth was reading a sixpenny Penguin. As they walked on, Pearson said that England was rapidly becoming an *Ile des Pingouins*. Much as the English loathed books, they had heard a lot about them, and here was a chance of doing something about it, and, anyway, it was only a tanner.

Eventually they fetched up at a roomy old bar, which was obviously the meeting-place of the relatively livelier sparks of the town, attracted no doubt by a pretty barmaid who was being assisted by an older one.

Pearson: This is a scene I have frequently contemplated with some melancholy. That elderly barmaid over there, once the focus of pop-eyed blokes like those, now has to work by the side of a girl—and a damned pretty one, too!—whose liver she would like to tear out. And yet, partly because it's her job and partly because her vanity still eggs her on, she has to drop cheery comments into the flow of amorous raillery, comments to which no one pays the slightest attention, except occasionally to brush one aside.

' But Heavenly Rosalind! '

The next morning Pearson and Kingsmill stepped out into an exquisitely beautiful winter day. There was a bright blue haze of smoke over the High Street, and the tall trees beyond were outlined against a translucent sky. Pearson having remarked that any one who travelled except on business at any time of the year except in the last week of January was a patent fool, they set forth towards Savernake Forest. As they climbed the slope, Kingsmill said that only the previous

Sunday he had seen a picture of the avenue in Savernake, and presumed that they were now approaching it. That glade, he said, was doubtless it. Very pretty, but hardly up to the photograph in the paper. All forests were alike—plenty of trees, that's what made them forests. Pearson expressed complete agreement.

Having traversed the glade, they strolled along through scattered trees. A man was approaching, pausing from time to time to look critically at a stump. Pearson suggested that they should accost him, and see what he had to say about it all. They did so, and learnt that he was a wood and forest surveyor. Among other things, he explained the method of telling a tree's age by its rings. How old were oaks, as a rule? asked Kingsmill. There was no rule, said the surveyor indulgently: an oak nine hundred years of age, and there were many in the forest, was nine hundred years old. It seemed quite a large forest, said Pearson. It certainly was, the surveyor replied, a little brusquely, adding that it wasn't altogether difficult to get lost in it. Pearson asked if the glade they had just left was the famous Avenue. 'Hardly!' he smiled. 'Now I'll tell you exactly how to get there.' He gave them detailed instructions, and they continued on their way, since nothing in the detailed instructions seemed to conflict with their doing so. Occasionally they caught glimpses of deer.

Pearson: This is a perfect setting for *As You Like It*. I have acted in it myself in a pastoral setting, but West Ealing, of course, is nothing to this. How I should love to produce it here! What a marvellous production it would be! Look at those trees! They are all just there for a production of *As You Like It*, and for no other conceivable purpose.

Kingsmill: What I love about *As You Like It* is that it couldn't possibly have been written by a wood and forest surveyor. The one man who is incapable of appreciating trees is the man who knows anything about them. It was just because Shakespeare used to lose and neglect the creeping hours of time under the shade of melancholy boughs that he was able to write like that, instead of being reduced to telling the reader how to compute the age of an oak. As he himself says:

'These earthly godfathers of heaven's lights
That give a name to every fixed star,
Have no more profit of their shining nights
Than those that walk and wot not what they are.'

Pearson (*continuing his own train of thought*)*:* But of course the sort of people who could afford to produce *As You* here are the sort of people who would make Savernake insupportable to any decent person, not that in such circumstances any decent person would be here to have Savernake made insupportable to him. Can't you see the audience? I've seen them at Stratford and Malvern—the Festival fan type.

Kingsmill: I was visualizing a more select audience, a country house party, with some one like Edmund Gosse to reconcile the lord of the manor to the intellectuals, and to convey to Gladys, Lady Savernake, after the intellectuals had been shipped back to London, their imperishable gratitude for having been allowed into the grounds on ostensibly equal terms.   One can imagine Gosse's letter:

'DEAR LADY GLADYS,
   'You will not, I know, expect me to be able to begin to tell you what these days have meant to me . . .' and so on down to 'Do believe me, dear Lady Gladys,
         Ever cordially and gratefully yours . . .'

Pearson: One sees why *As You* is so popular with rich people, with its pretty young aristocrats, male and female, gambolling innocently about in Arcadia. Shakespeare had reached the point in his life when he was utterly sick of the aristocracy, and of playing up to them, but couldn't bring himself to cut his losses.

Kingsmill: And so he is more maudlin about them than in the earlier plays when he was really admiring them.   I think he identified himself with that faithful old ass Adam, a part he actually played. A person is always sentimental when he is suppressing what he feels in favour of what he would like to feel.

Pearson: And it wasn't only the aristocracy he was sentimentalizing; it was women, too.   The black mistress of the sonnets diluted into Rosalind!

   'Thus must I from the smoke into the smother,
   From tyrant duke unto a tyrant brother—
   But *heavenly* Rosalind!'

A startled deer disappeared into the undergrowth. They emerged on to a grass patch near the road, and were about to give up the search for the Avenue when, glancing to their right, they saw beyond stone gates trees much higher than any they had yet encountered. 'What on earth's that?' Pearson exclaimed. As they passed through the gates, there stretched before them a double row of immensely high trees running in a straight line for what seemed three or four miles. It resembled an aisle in some superhuman cathedral, and the winter sun was shining through the upper branches as though through the narrow windows of a clerestory. They walked silently along for about a mile, and then returned. On emerging from the forest, they saw beyond Marlborough the Wiltshire downs, dotted with clumps of trees on the distant horizon. Descending to the town, they had lunch in the St. Patrick tea rooms, packed and got into the Swindon bus, after a final stroll along the still sun-drenched High Street.

Bath, Brighton and Oxford

At Swindon, which held nothing to detain them, they took the train for Bristol. As they were approaching Bath, Kingsmill asked Pearson for his opinion of it.

Pearson: It's a marvellous place to think about, but hardly a place to live in.

Kingsmill: Yes, there are too many associations. At a distance one can choose what association one likes at the moment—Jane Austen, or Smollett, or Winkle running round the Crescent, or Sheridan's lovely wife, but when you're in the place there's Goldsmith on your left, and Nash on your right, and Clive just behind you, and Burke just in front. . . .

Pearson: With Mrs. Thrale at square leg, Sydney Smith at point, Chatham at long stop, and Johnson in the slips. All the same, a wonderful city, the quintessence of eighteenth century architecture, and the most attractive residential town in England except Brighton—those charming Regency streets running up from Marine Parade with their balconies and little bow windows, in which one pictures pretty girls with short directory sleeves sitting at their spinets.

Kingsmill: The impossibility of picturing Oxford as inhabited by anything but pot-bellied portswilling professors if one's thinking of the eighteenth century, or twentieth century dons if one's thinking of the twentieth, may explain why it always gives me a feeling of surprise when people rave over it as the most beautiful place in England. I shall never care for it. I didn't like it the first time I went there, and I didn't like it the last.

Dutch Bulbs

It was dark and rainy when they reached Bristol, and Temple Meads station looked cavernous and desolate, unaccountably recalling to both travellers the stations from which they had set forth in the last war. As they trailed through the subway each tried to remember all the fascinating associations which had betrayed them into visiting this drear necropolis. 'We'll go to the nearest possible pub,' said Pearson, 'so as to make a quick getaway in the morning.'

They put up at, and with, a hotel not very far from the station. It was, they learned from their waitress at dinner, which they had by themselves in a pleasant enough room upstairs, the headquarters of, among others, gentlemen travelling in Dutch bulbs. Spalding, she said, used to be the centre of that business, but as Lincolnshire was certain to be bombed if there was war, they were looking for somewhere safe, and that's why they'd come to Bristol.

Descending to the smoking-room after dinner, Pearson and Kingsmill were able to study the bulb travellers at close quarters. Two in especial attracted their attention. One of them was sitting on a small sofa by the fire, the other was rigid on a chair behind the sofa, over the top of which their conversation, in Dutch, was carried on. It was practically a monologue, the Dutchman on the sofa going on and on in a monotone which every now and then rose into a fluty shriek, upon which the rigid Dutchman, whose face was a mask of suppressed loathing, turned sharply towards him, discharged a rasping rattling fusillade, and jerking his head back again resumed his look of implacable hatred.

Chatterton

'The interior of St. Mary Redcliff and the exterior of Salisbury Cathedral are the most beautiful objects in the world,' said Pearson the next morning, as he conducted his friend through the slums between their hotel and St. Mary. 'People talk of the Taj Mahal—Tcha!'

It was snowing hard as they passed Chatterton's home, and the white roofs intensified the gloom of the dark houses beneath.

Kingsmill: I have always wished to read Chatterton, or rather that I had read Chatterton. Everything about him, except his works and himself, interests me.

Pearson: That applies to quite a good few people, to any one in fact who is at the beginning of some movement, and fizzles out quickly enough to be adopted as its patron saint. . . .

Kingsmill: Or patron sinner, as with Horst-Wessel, the Nazi Rouget de Lisle. Chatterton was the Rouget de Lisle of the Romantic Movement. Hence Wordsworth's fine outburst:

'I thought of Chatterton, the marvellous boy,
The sleepless soul that perished in its pride . . .'

I don't feel that's really about Chatterton. It's about. . . .
Pearson: Wordsworth.

St. Mary Redcliff

Pearson presented the interior of the church to his friend with modest pride. After walking round, they sat for some time at the west end of the nave. 'The whole thing gives the impression of not only soaring upwards, but also of flowing along,' said Kingsmill. Pearson hushed him, and they continued to sit in silence.

Rising, Pearson told Kingsmill he must come up with him to the Muniment Room, so as to have a good view of Bristol city. Having toiled up, and nothing being visible through the snowstorm, they came down again. As they walked away, Pearson expatiated on the glories of Gothic. Only a Goth, he said, would tolerate any other kind of architecture. 'Think of Wren,' he exclaimed, 'after what we've just been looking at!' Kingsmill did not altogether agree. 'I don't care for Renaissance architecture, generally speaking,' he said. 'Dreary as Rome is as a whole, St. Peter's is the dreariest thing in it. But St. Paul's is the most wonderful thing even in London—that marvellous view of it from Fleet Street, and that other from Westminster Bridge. . . .'

Pearson: Or the perfect glimpse from Whitehall.

Kingsmill nodded, a little doubtfully, but recovering himself concluded: 'And above and beyond everything else, St. Paul's from Hampstead Heath.'

Marshfield

Pearson and Kingsmill had been invited by their friends, John and Clement Davenport, to spend a night at Marshfield on the Cotswolds, so on returning to the hotel they asked Howard, the boots, where the Chippenham buses started. He was a simple friendly boy, and gave them much information, all of which turned out to be inexact. This was perhaps because his mind was revolving other matters. It was his evening off, he told them; Jim and he had alternate afternoons and evenings. It would probably, he thought, be raining all the afternoon, but he expected it to be fine by six o'clock. As it was not yet three, this did not cheer the travellers much, but they set out and, following Howard's instructions, found themselves wading through a square which was exposed to the full blast of the storm and was nowhere near where the bus started. After holding up several peevish pedestrians, they at last got to the bus, forty minutes before it was due to leave. They climbed in.

> *Pearson:* I am beginning to understand, Hugh, why you are no longer a tourist agent.
>
> *Kingsmill:* And I have always understood why you have never been one.

The bus, at last jerking itself into motion, sideslipped

through the slushy streets, but as it emerged into the country and began to climb up between white fields in the gathering twilight, peace descended upon the inmates.

Pearson: John told me that their home was very high up on the Cotswolds.

Kingsmill: How high up?

Pearson: At least seven hundred feet above sea-level.

Kingsmill: As I have spent a good deal of my life in Switzerland, making large sums for my father's

tourist agency, you will forgive me if I am not impressed. To reach a height of seven hundred feet above sea-level in Switzerland, it would be necessary to get into a diver's suit and descend to the bottom of Lake Geneva.

The bus set them down at the Crown, Marshfield, where they took refuge from the storm which was rising again, and stoked up on buttered toast, scones, jam and cakes before setting out in search of their friends. It was blowing a blizzard as they came out of the Crown and their feet sank deep into the snow. Ploughing along the dark street, they felt like two travellers in one of Scott's romances as the wind whirled great clouds of snow off the roofs and chimneys. 'Beshrew me,' said the taller of the two travellers, ''tis ill faring on such a hell-brew night as this!' 'God send Messer Davenport be not from home!' muttered his companion.

Their destination, The Malt House, was on the main street, and they were greatly cheered, coming in out of the blizzard, by the warm and roomy study into which they were shown. The maid said that Mr. and Mrs. Davenport would be back from Bath shortly, and had

left word that they were to make themselves at home; and this, with a bottle of whisky brought in by the maid, they did so thoroughly that when their host and hostess arrived the travellers called to them not to stand on ceremony, but to come right in and have a drink.

John and Clement Davenport were recently back from Hollywood, where John had been writing film scenarios. John was under thirty, Clement in the early twenties, and though they naturally felt a good deal older than Pearson and Kingsmill, they had never rubbed it in during an acquaintance which had extended over some years.

The travellers were snow-bound on the following day,

and spent a second night at Marshfield. Comparing views with John, they gathered that he did not care for Keats. The *Ode to the Nightingale*, he said, sounded very nice, but wasn't it a Cockney's dream? 'This,' he said, 'is how it ought to be read:

> 'My 'eart ikes and a drowsy numbness pines
> My sense as though of 'emlock I 'ad drunk
> Or emptied some dull opiate to the drines. . . .'

His reading was so amusing that they were nonplussed, but pulling himself together Kingsmill said that any poet could be burlesqued in such a manner. John denied this, and Kingsmill having tried and failed to cockneyfy Shelley's *Skylark* and Wordsworth's *Ode* admitted that there might be something in John's feeling about Keats.

There was a grand piano in the long room upstairs, and Pearson asked John to play some Beethoven. He consented indulgently, but having played a Sonata asked Pearson if he would mind a little Bach. Pearson said he wouldn't mind a *very* little Bach, but presumed that John in common with all right-minded people played other composers only in order to enjoy the return to Beethoven. John saying nothing, Kingsmill, whose views were the same as Pearson's, pressed for a reply; but John, smiling pleasantly, began to play Bach.

At Kingsmill's request, Clement showed him a portfolio of her drawings, which he had never yet seen. 'But these are extraordinary! These are amazing!' he kept on exclaiming. 'I've never seen anything that gets the atmosphere of dreams better—the loneliness, the endless distances. This is genius!' Clement sitting impassively by his side, he felt that she was not taking his enthusiasm seriously enough. 'I really mean it!' he said querulously, and turned appealingly to John and Pearson, who ceased their conversation for a moment, and then resumed it.

The post arrived, bringing a letter for Clement which caused her and John a good deal of annoyance. 'The cheek of it!' she exclaimed. 'I wish the little squit was here!' and clenching her fist she swung back her long and shapely arm, looking like Athene about to put paid to the account of some impertinent mortal.

At breakfast on the following morning, referring to this letter, she said in a reflective tone: 'It's the first time any person has ever picked a quarrel with me in my life.'

'The brute!' cried Kingsmill. 'It's too bad. What a cad he must be!'

'Of course,' she added musingly, 'I've picked hundreds of quarrels with other people.'

Pikes and Butter

The buses were running again on Friday morning, and the travellers set off for Chippenham, where they took a car for Cirencester. On the way their attention was caught by some enormous barn-like buildings on the flat table-land, and they asked the driver about them, wondering whether they might be a feature of the Cotswold landscape. 'They're aerodromes,' said the driver. 'They're putting up a lot of them round here.

There's plenty of flat country, and it's out of the way. I suppose we'll want 'em.'

At Cirencester they went to the King's Head. In the lounge, having tea by the fire, there was a tall friendly-looking young fellow, with whom they fell into conversation, and learnt that he was a naval lieutenant attached to the Air Force. Above the fireplace hung a large oil painting, representing an episode in the history of Cirencester, in August 1642. An angry crowd in the market-place outside the King's Head, armed with pikes and cudgels, was storming a coach, out of which a gentleman in cavalier costume was stepping with a perturbed expression; and with reason, for the cavalier in question, Lord Chandos, in attempting to collect soldiers for Charles I had, as he was just beginning to realize, succeeded in raising an armed force for the other side.

The peer's further adventures were recorded beneath the picture: his carriage was torn to pieces, some of his companions were killed, and he himself escaped into the King's Head. It was the first bloodshed of the Civil War.

'Rather an interesting picture, that,' said Kingsmill to the naval lieutenant.

'Oh, yes, it's a good picture,' he replied. 'This was once the dining-room, and we used to flick pats of butter at it. It was a good thing to have bets on. That chap in the middle was the bull's-eye, and so he got most of the blobs. Of course every one knows the picture here, and the landlord didn't seem to think our treatment was improving it.'

'So I suppose that's why this is no longer the dining-room,' suggested Pearson.

'That's probably it,' he agreed with a smile.

Remembering the aerodromes they had passed on the way, Pearson and Kingsmill wanted to know what the Air Force thought of things in general. Were they anxious about Germany? The lieutenant didn't seem anxious about anything except whether some friends he was expecting from Southampton would arrive safely that evening.

'Safely?' queried Kingsmill. 'Are they flying?'

'Oh no, they're coming by car, but there are forty-three pubs on the road.'

After tea they went out into the market-place, which, except for the welcome absence of Lord Chandos's recruits, exactly resembled, with the beautiful church in the background, the painting they had just been looking at. They walked up the main street. Everything was calm and old in the evening light, and they felt tranquil and remote.

Late that evening they were drinking their whiskies in the lounge when the naval lieutenant came in with his friends. There were four of them, all in a condition which justified his earlier anxiety about their safe arrival. It had clearly been a near thing. On seeing Pearson and Kingsmill by the fire, the lieutenant paused, and swaying slightly indicated his companions with a deprecating gesture, murmuring: 'These are my friends.' Nodding perfunctorily at Pearson and Kingsmill, the others dropped heavily into chairs here and there, and called for drink. The lieutenant explained to them that it was past closing time, and they must have drinks on him. Raising no objection, they named their drinks, which were brought after some parley with the manageress, who, however, was compelled to yield on the technical issue.

Spirited if sporadic talk bubbled up from them. The liveliest and most coherent member was a young farmer, slight and neatly dressed, with quick dark eyes. He was from the neighbouring district, and had no doubt gone forth with the naval lieutenant to meet the rest, perhaps finding them in or near the thirty-fourth pub on the Southampton-Cirencester road. There was some sparring between him and a heavy youth who from time to time stared balefully at Pearson and Kingsmill, and

from his look seemed ready to fight with any one. His grievance against the farmer was that one had to wade through sewage to get into his place. The sewage, said the other, was there to keep him out. This stymied him for a time, but eventually after some muttering he articulated: 'Nothing annoys me more than trying to milk a cow.' 'And nothing annoys a cow more than trying to be milked by you,' rejoined the farmer.

Pearson and Kingsmill burst into laughter at this

retort, and the lout looked at them so menacingly that the lieutenant interposed with: 'It's all right. They're ex-Service.' He indicated Pearson and Kingsmill. 'We'll be like that later.' This solemn prospect had a tranquillizing effect on the other, the talk evaporated with the drink, and they stumbled off to bed, followed thoughtfully by Pearson and Kingsmill.

Fairford

The next morning, Saturday January 28, they set off for Fairford in a bus. The sun was shining; there was a faint haze over the white fields, and Kingsmill remarked that the snow, as always in England, was looking rather sheepish, as much as to say: 'I know I made a bit of a nuisance of myself earlier this week, but it's not really like me, and I'm just going.'

At Fairford, under pressure from Pearson, they went into a pub, where the strata of country society was presented to their view—a squire's son who accepted the deference of the others without seeming to enjoy it, a self-assertive farmer who was deferential against the grain, a solicitor who deferred automatically, and a nonentity who deferred naturally.

Before going into the church, Pearson pointed to the gates leading into a large park, and said: 'Sydney Smith often went through those gates when he was tired of shepherding his flock on Salisbury Plain and wanted to sample the venison of his patron, Hicks Beach, one of those landowning plutocrats who regulated English Christianity in the age of reason.'

The church had a beautiful west window of many colours, red predominating. 'I'm glad *that* escaped the Civil War—one thing at any rate that Archbishop Laud missed!' Pearson cried.

'Laud? Wasn't Cromwell the church wrecker of that time?'

'He may have been, but they were all in it. Rival firms—there's nothing to pick and choose between the opposing thugs of any age. All one can be sure of is the continuity of thuggery.'

'When thieves fall out, another lot falls in.'

Further large generalizations might have followed, but for the scene which met their eyes as they emerged from the church. The haze over the meadows had dissolved, the sun was shining in a cloudless sky, and innumerable bright rivulets of melting snow were running across their path. They took the road for Bibury, a high table-land stretching away to either side.

Falstaff's Ghost

Kingsmill: This is the kind of day, and this was the country, in which Shakespeare was at his happiest.

Pearson: Though neither he nor any one else since the world began has ever seen such a glorious January morning as this.

Kingsmill: Well, at any rate, it was round about

here that he first tasted the uncertain glory of an April day.

Pearson: And the certain glory of a summer one, for it was out of his summers that Falstaff was born, and it is on the Cotswolds that Falstaff is at his richest.

Kingsmill: Couldn't we group our book—whatever it turns out to be about, and whatever publisher it may eventually interest—round Falstaff, more or less?

Pearson: Have you ever had the smallest doubt that this book is going to be about Falstaff, the whole of Falstaff, and nothing but Falstaff?

Kingsmill: We might call it *Falstaff's Ghost*. With all these aerodromes going up, England is undoubtedly coming out of its coma, and . . .

Pearson: And about time, too—with English Prime Ministers running like office boys to Rome and Berchtesgaden, and English Foreign Secretaries accepting it as in the order of things that English subjects should be debagged by Oriental scum.

Kingsmill: Falstaff's Ghost would symbolize something permanent in the English character. Admittedly, Sir John doesn't typify the actual man-at-arms, but whenever there's fighting in the foreground, he's applauding in the background, and as the warriors come back for a drink, he moves into the centre of the picture.

Pearson: And his humour is the quality in Englishmen which gives them the balance and therefore the staying power which—I speak in all moderation —puts them at the top and crown of all civilized peoples; not that there ever have been any except the English.

Kingsmill: A ghost with a burning face and a huge belly smiling benevolently down on the forty-three pubs between Southampton and Cirencester —it would make a wonderful book jacket.

Pearson: How quickly the snow is melting under this sun—there's quite a large dab of green already over there. These are obviously the fields of which Falstaff babbled on his death-bed.

Kingsmill: I'm afraid that's Theobald's idea of Falstaff's end, not Shakespeare's. It was a brilliant emendation of his, but I remember being completely convinced by Darrell Figgis's case for the original reading—'And his nose was as sharp as a pen and a table of green fels.' Figgis maintained that 'and' was a misprint for 'on', and that a goose-quill against a background of green felt was exactly how Shakespeare would have seen Falstaff's nose growing sharp and white in death.

Pearson: Figgis is right. I like the green fields passage, but it's not really Shakespeare or Falstaff.

Coln St. Aldwyn

They had reached the top of the slope leading down into Coln St. Aldwyn, and saw below them a shining expanse of flooded meadows stretching to a dark bank which rose steeply out of the water and was crowned by a line of trees very black against the brilliant winter sky. As they gazed down, Pearson muttering 'incredible' under his breath, their attention was caught by a statuesque horse in the middle of a field near the village.

Pearson: A little self-conscious, that horse, I think.

Kingsmill: Yes. The observed of two observers.

Pearson:

'O what a noble mind is here o'erthrown,
 The courtier's, soldier's, scholar's, eye, tongue, sword;
 The expectancy and rose of the fair state,
 The glass of fashion and the mould of form,
 The observed of all observers, quite, quite down.'

How I used to love that passage, and mouth it at home after playing the fourth or fifth citizen in *Julius Caesar* at His Majesty's. Hamlet containing within himself all the enviable attributes of mankind, being not only an Admirable Crichton and the cynosure of all eyes, but also misunderstood and undervalued by every one about him, no wonder every actor has always seen himself in the part and longed to play it. They have forced it down the public's throat for three hundred years, and done it with such delirious enthusiasm for themselves that the public out of sheer inertia have accepted the play as the greatest ever written. . . .

Kingsmill: And Hamlet as a profound mystery, when he is only a complicated mystification.

Pearson: Of course, one must remember that Falstaff was three or four years behind Shakespeare when he wrote *Hamlet.* He was going down into the pit at the bottom of which he was to find *Timon of Athens.*

They were walking along by the shining flooded

31

fields, and Pearson exclaimed: 'We are now about to enter the most beautiful village street in the kingdom.' They turned left, and as they went up the street had to admit that though very pleasant, and humanized by two kindly dogs, it did not fulfil the expectations aroused by the approach. Indeed, a third dog making a pass at them further on, they conceded that Coln St. Aldwyn on an ordinary day might be quite an ordinary place.

The Goose and the Peg

Kingsmill: By the way, I know we're on the Cotswolds, but isn't the part Shakespeare was familiar with some distance off—Chipping Campden, and those places near Stratford?

Pearson: He must have known the whole of this country, but probably the place he knew best was Dursley in the western Cotswolds. The Shallow scenes in the second part of *Henry IV* have several references to that neighbourhood.

Kingsmill: Oughtn't we to make for Dursley, and

then follow the road he must have travelled between there and Stratford?

Pearson: That must keep till some publisher is prepared to materialize Falstaff's ghost.

Kingsmill: I'm not much looking forward to Stratford itself. My chief memory of it is a week or so in the summer of 1919. In the spring of that year the Mayor, Archibald Flower, went up to London to see my father, who as an organizer of winter sports and summer cruises and so on seemed the

right man to bring into being a War Memoria which would give Stratford a leg-up on the business side. At that time I was parked on my uncle Holdsworth, who was running those Scotch hotels where you and I had such a pleasant time the summer before last. There was a general feeling both in the northern and southern branches of the business that I should be happier elsewhere, and my father, on hearing the word 'Shakespeare' from Flower, by a false association of ideas thought that I should be happiest of all in Stratford. He had a very quick and fertile mind, and before Flower had properly grasped the, to him, unimportant fact of my existence, he found that the Stratford War Memorial had defined itself in my father's imagination as a vast hostel for American

visitors, managed by Sir Henry Lunn's second son.
As a minor issue my father was prepared to safe-
guard Stratford itself, at that time threatened by
a strong Bolshevik element which wanted to erect
factories and get rid of Shakespeare, whose birth-
place some of the extremists had recently tried to
storm. So he formed a Stratford-on-Avon
Preservation Committee, to protect the natural
beauties and old Tudor buildings of the town,
and generally to make Stratford 'an abiding
monument to the memory of its greatest citizen'.

The Town Council, predominantly Bolshevik
or at least anti-Tudor, was hostile to this enterprise, and convened an extraordinary meeting,
which my father was invited to attend. In a
circular asking the public to subscribe one
hundred thousand pounds towards a Stratford
War Memorial, my father had referred to Stratford
as 'the Mecca of every Englishman', but on the
chairman of the Town Council asking him the
date of his first visit to this Mecca, he had to
name a day in the previous month.

Meanwhile the financial response to my father's
appeal was proving meagre, for people were getting
rather tired of putting money into the pockets of
the living in order to testify their gratitude to
the dead. My father was accustomed to being
the most enthusiastic member of his own com-
mittees. Inertia in the rest he could understand
and even sympathize with, but what he did not
like was an actively obstructive member, on this
occasion Sir Sidney Lee, who as the official Shakespearean of the day knew with some precision how

much Shakespeare could be made to yield, and would therefore have been mistrustful of untried and hazardous experiments, even if they had been undertaken with the aim of benefiting Sir Sidney Lee.

With the public listless, and the committee unhelpful, my welcome at Stratford when I arrived from Scotland was a little languid. However, Flower asked me to dinner one evening, before a performance of *Julius Caesar*. The producer, by the way, was Bridges Adams, whom I think you know. We had seen a good deal of one another at Oxford, and during my stay in Stratford we had some refreshing talks, on matters remote from Stratford.

Sir Johnston Forbes-Robertson, William Archer and Harold Child were stopping with Flower, and I returned with them after the play. At dinner, with the performance still to come, the talk had flagged, but now at supper they were in a relaxed and amiable mood, greeting Forbes-Robertson's 'What a fellow Shakespeare was! He knew his mob—ha! ha! ha!' with a gracious acquiescence which allowed Shakespeare, in spite of everything, to be as experienced and knowledgeable as themselves.

As Stratford was packed for the Festival, I was lodged in a huge building with between two and three hundred elementary school teachers of the other sex, whom Cecil Sharp, the Morris Dance and Folk Lore resurrectionist, had, by some means or other, trepanned into sacrificing their holidays to the business of recapturing movements and sounds which had welled spontaneously out of the yokels of the Middle Ages. I had tea with Cecil Sharp, a small, unsmiling man, and at his suggestion witnessed a Morris Dance practice in the stone yard of a Council School—about a dozen women teachers in doublet and hose, one of them white-haired and very decrepit, leaping in conformity with the boundings of a shrill-voiced young man, who from time to time let out cries purporting to convey mirth on a village green.

One afternoon I called on the vicar, the Reverend Melville, with whom I discussed the anti-Shakespearean feeling on the Town Council. He was a large heavily-built man, not very articulate. 'They don't seem to realize,' he said in slow protesting tones, 'that they're killing the goose which lays the golden eggs.'

Sometimes in the mornings I used to visit the Shakespeare Memorial Library, where I got to know the librarian. We were talking one day about Sir Sidney Lee and Sir Israel Gollancz; and on my remarking that I always thought of these two as Shylock's Revenge, he said: 'Well, Shakespeare's a very good peg to hang one's hat on.'

When I wanted a talk with the founder of the Shakespeare Head Press, A. H. Bullen, who loved Shakespeare and was himself a poet, I used to go to a pleasant old inn over the way from his Press. All his energy and enthusiasm had gone into the Press, but now he was content to leave it to his devoted assistants, the Miss Listers. He had spent a large part of his life in Stratford, and was rather tired.

Kingsmill ceased, and they walked on in silence for a short time.

Pearson: But what about your father's enterprise? What happened to it?

Kingsmill: Only five hundred pounds of the hundred thousand came in. Later, I have heard, Flower went to America, where the combination of Stratford's leading citizen and Stratford's greatest citizen proved more fruitful than over here.

Memories of Stratford

Pearson: My own memories of Stratford are rather more variegated than yours. I was very young when I first knew it. From the ages of six to twelve I used to spend my Christmas holidays at the house of my grandfather, who for some forty years was vicar of Ettington, about four miles out. When I tell you that I played there as a child, I don't expect you to be thrilled, but when I add that one of my playgrounds was Ettington Park, in the housekeeper's room of which lay, as yet undiscovered, the commonplace book of Dean Swift, one of the greatest finds in our history, perhaps your literary and financial sense will be aroused. Day after day within a yard or two of my unwitting wits! To pass to less painful themes, I recall a large children's party at the house of a cousin at Clifford Chambers, where Michael Drayton used to live. While we were playing, there was a sudden spate of women, one of whom, in a very frilly flouncy dress, swooped down upon me, and submerged me like a descending balloon. Later some one told me that I had been kissed by Marie Corelli. Why she picked me out in particular, I don't know.

Kingsmill: It takes all sorts to make a world.

Pearson: My next memory is much later, and links up with your experiences at Stratford. For two years, from 1912 to 1914, I was secretary of a Shakespearean Society, the motto of which ran: 'Using no other weapon but his name.' Actually it made Shakespeare palatable to the public by associating him with every eminent name it could nobble, from royal princesses to continental professors. Theoretically the Society had branches all over the world. Picture then the intense surprise of London headquarters, which consisted of the Hon. Director, Acton Bond, and myself, when a gentleman turned up one day and informed us that he was a vice-president of a branch in New Zealand. We knew there was an individual in New Zealand who called himself the secretary of a branch, and we were grateful to this solitary lunatic, as I presumed him to be, for having a form of lunacy which suited the imperial aims and objects of our note-paper. But that was all. Acton Bond, who had had many calls on his self-possession, was the first to recover, and our visitor's reception clearly came up to what he had expected of the Mother Country at this solemn moment.

Thenceforward at every meeting of the Society

he appeared on the platform as an important imperial representative. He was made to distribute prizes, and he was glad to deliver speeches, and finally he and a large wreath were escorted by Acton Bond and myself to Stratford, where the wreath was laid on Shakespeare's grave, the papers the next morning coming out with 'Distinguished New Zealander pays tribute to Shakespeare'.

By the way, the first President of the Society was your pal Sidney Lee.

Kingsmill: And how did he get on with Acton Bond?

Pearson: About as well as he got on with your father. There's a story that Edward VII once said to him: 'Stick to Shakespeare, Mr. Lee, there's money in him,' and, as you also noticed, Lee didn't want this royal tip to be taken by any one except himself. However, Bond got the better of Lee, though he was less fortunate with Lee's opposite number on the Continent, Dr. Georg Brandes. One of the most uncomfortable moments in my life occurred when Brandes came over from Copenhagen to lecture to our Society. The difference between Brandes and Lee was that Brandes was interested in Shakespeare as well as in himself, and so was not at his happiest when he was on his Shakespearean tours. I shouldn't go so far as to say he loved Shakespeare, but he certainly loathed every one connected with him.

Acton Bond, socially a charming man, with a perfectly produced and agreeably modulated voice, was sitting with Brandes and me before the lecture in the green room of the Garrick Theatre. *Othello* was Bond's favourite play, and very impressively he used to read the leading part. 'I was greatly interested, master, in your statement that *King Lear* was Shakespeare's greatest work,' he said to Brandes, who was nursing his pointed beard and gazing coldly into space. 'But surely you place *Othello* on an equal eminence?'

'I do not.'

This held Bond for a space, and his eye circled the room, resting on me for a moment. Then, composing himself, he turned to Brandes again. 'Well, I suppose—ha, ha—I suppose it's a matter of taste.'

'It is not.'

Kingsmill: What on earth did Bond do?

Pearson: Left the room. And I wished I could follow him.

Kingsmill: And what did Brandes do?

Pearson: Remained motionless, still nursing his pointed beard and gazing coldly into space. The whole thing was as embarrassing as anything I can remember.

Maupassant—in English

Kingsmill: A very embarrassing thing once happened to a friend of mine, who used to write short stories for the *Strand* before the last war. He was always lamenting the restrictions laid on English short story writers in those days; and any happening with any touch of impropriety in it would wring from him the cry: 'Maupassant! If only it could be done in English!' So perhaps, in some obscure way, he invited his doom.

He was returning to England from Muerren, and got into the train for Boulogne at Interlaken. Having a long journey before him, he was pleased to find a really lovely girl in the corner seat opposite his. Composing himself in a meditative attitude, he gazed out into the twilight with the air of a man whose natural sweetness had, if anything, been deepened by many and varied trials. To make himself perfectly comfortable for a situation which, from a slight smile the girl gave him, he hoped might develop favourably, he rose gracefully and went into the corridor, quickening his steps as soon as he was out of sight. On returning, he settled himself in his  previous attitude, with a courteous apology to the girl for disturbing her. A minute later a guard wrenched the door open, and in harsh guttural English taxed my friend with breaking the regulations by using the lavatory while the train was at rest. My friend tried to shoo him away with dismissive gestures, but the guard, producing a receipt book, stated that the fine was five francs, and while my friend was fumbling for the money made out a receipt.

The girl was smiling, a little more widely than before, but my friend did not gaze out into the twilight again.

Theseus at Bibury

They had reached a dip in the road, and went down between wooded glades into Bibury. As they approached the village, they perceived a number of people running excitedly in one direction, and pointing as they ran. The horn of a huntsman sounded clearly through the still air, and coming out into the open they saw the hounds drawing a cover on the slope beyond a stream. Between trees the scarlet coats of huntsmen flashed by. The fox darted into and out of view, a shrill cry went up from the villagers, and a bellowing came down from the slope. To the surprise of Kingsmill, his friend, purple in the face, strode along the village street, muttering loud imprecations which went unnoticed in the general commotion, except by a lady who was following the hunt and stepped back in alarm as Pearson's voice rose into a roar.

On their left was a lake, formed by the recent floods, and Kingsmill remarked how delightful a row of old Tudor cottages looked with the water lapping their steps. Pearson yielding to the soothing effect of the sunlight on the water, and the soft old brick, Kingsmill ventured to suggest that a hunt had its picturesque side, appreciated by Shakespeare himself, who had given Theseus some of the most beautiful lines in *A Midsummer Night's Dream* :

'My hounds are bred out of the Spartan kind,
  So flew'd, so sanded; and their heads are hung
  With ears that sweep away the morning dew . . .

. . . A cry more tuneable
Was never holla'd to, nor cheered with horn,
In Crete, in Sparta, nor in Thessaly.'

They went into a delightful sunny hotel, and over a delicious tea Kingsmill taxed Pearson with having covered a nostalgia for his fox-hunting youth with an outburst of exaggerated spleen. 'Possibly,' said Pearson, and knitted his brows in thought as he piled jam on a thickly-buttered scone. The scone devoured, Pearson took another, and while buttering it said: 'There are two types of men who get my goat; those who damn the sins they have a mind to, and those who damn the sins they have no mind to. The first is the puritan who suppresses his natural instincts, and whose sex goes rancid within him. Of such was W. T. Stead. The second is the ex-rake and debauchee who after a life-time of guzzling like a hog, drinking like a fish, and copulating like a stoat, turns over a new leaf when he can no longer gorge, soak and womanize, and preaches temperance, sobriety and chastity. Of such was Tolstoy. Compared with these two, the idiot of a fox-hunter strikes me as a relatively harmless cad.'

'A powerful speech, but haven't you rather confused the issue?'

'I hope so.'

Twilight

After tea they turned homewards, taking the road to Cirencester. On the outskirts of the village there was a cottage with a plaque on it bearing the words *Gloucestershire Police Station*. 'Surely a small headquarters for a whole county?' queried Kingsmill. 'Probably put up by the local Dogberry, and inhabited by the local Verges,' replied Pearson. 'One of the minor mysteries of life,' murmured Kingsmill. 'To us,' said Pearson, 'if to no one else.'

The evening haze was rising, and the sun showed through it like a great red ball. As they walked in the gathering twilight, they noticed on the further side of a large field a white object which puzzled them. Was it an opening in a hedge, they wondered, or a whitewashed shed, or a solitary tree blasted by lightning, or a war memorial, or a paralysed cow? Unable to bear the uncertainty any longer, Pearson waded through a ditch into the field, and presently returned with the information that it was a white horse.

'This is a field day for horses,' said Kingsmill.

'But definitely over now,' said Pearson, detaching lumps of mud from his trousers.

In the dusk rooks were circling round a tall clump of trees a little ahead of them.

Pearson: How often Shakespeare must have seen them circling like that on these uplands! 'Light thickens, and the crow makes wing to the rooky woods. Good things of day begin to droop and drowse.'

Kingsmill: From that speech onwards *Macbeth* is all darkness—the pure night of the soul which has abandoned everything for power. *Lear* is different —the darkness there is rent by lightning, which shows the heaven the old man sees by flashes as his obsession with power falls from him.

Pearson: *Macbeth* is the black ocean in which Elizabeth and Essex drowned. In *Lear* it is Shakespeare himself who is trying to get to land, out of the sea into which he plunged in his youth.

They came to the village of Barnsley, where lights were twinkling through the latticed windows, and they thought of the villages all over England with their little points of light shining through the darkness. From a high bank, as they walked on, some cows, outlined against the faint sky, stared down at them implacably, yet with a tinge of disquietude, as though they were feeling that the existence of human beings made faith very difficult.

Kingsmill suggested that if a bus came along they should take it. They jogged on, and presently perceived some shadowy figures shifting about at the side of the road. 'If Shakespeare were here,' said Pearson, 'he wouldn't like the look of those people. He'd assume they were footpads.' To Kingsmill's relief the figures were waiting for the bus, of which he had been beginning to despair, and soon they were straphanging their way into Cirencester.

After dinner, as they were resting in the lounge, they did not feel equal to demurring on being asked if the wireless might be turned on for a speech by Neville Chamberlain at a banquet in Birmingham. He appeared to be reassuring a number of business men. There were, he said, various signs 'which seemed to show that the recession of last year had passed its peak'. 'And that,' said Kingsmill, 'is the kind of prose style for which the English pay a man ten thousand a year.' The Prime Minister then turned to the international situation, and, inhaling deeply, quavered forth 'We must be stro-o-ong'. 'Thank God,' said Pearson, '*that's* not the strength we are going to draw on now.'

A Publess Village

Sunday was cold and grey. Feeling rather flat after the marvellous day before, they drifted out on the western road before lunch. 'This,' said Pearson, 'is the sort of day that gets the mood in which Shakespeare wrote his last plays:

'Jog on, jog on, the footpath way
And merrily hent the stile-a,
Your sad heart tires all the way,
Your merry goes a mile-a.'

At the last line he broke into a shuffling trot, and his mouth widened in a wretched grin.

'Those last two lines,' said Kingsmill, 'are an improvement on the original:

> 'A merry heart goes all the day,
> Your sad tires in a mile-a.

'Your version seems more poignant to me, and more in keeping with his broken-down mood, in which it would seem an achievement to cover as much as a mile. The "jog" sets the note. No one jogs joyfully.'

They passed by dreary frozen fields, turned left off the main road and came to an old grey village. Feeling hungry they looked about for a pub, and were informed by the only person visible in the main street that there was no pub in the place, but that they could probably get a bottle of beer at the village shop. Having obtained beer, chocolate and biscuits, and learnt that the name of the village was Daglinworth, they peered round for some shelter in which to eat, but finding none went up a hill towards the church, everything seeming inexpressibly old, as if a Witanegemot or some similar Anglo-Saxon pastime might be met with round any corner.

Having looked into the church, they seated themselves in the porch, Pearson in recalcitrant mood picturing the squire as a petty tyrant whose own cellars were sweating liquor of every kind, while his wretched villagers, if any spark of life remained to be extinguished in them, had to run to the nearest pub in Cirencester with their tongues hanging out. The travellers ate and drank, if eating and drinking it could be called, and leaving the precincts of the church went down the hill, on their way passing the vicarage, through the windows of which they beheld the vicar and his family happily assembled round a groaning board.

After tea Kingsmill went in search of a Shakespeare. The proprietor of the King's Head was guarded and non-committal, his manner implying that no immediate steps would be taken, but that Kingsmill and his friend could consider themselves as henceforth under observation. Somewhat ruffled, Kingsmill returned to Pearson. 'Of course,' he said, 'it's all one can expect in a country where "putting ideas into people's heads" is looked upon as a subversive practice, and where a man who has lost his mind is called "mental", though no one's called physical on his death-bed, or moral in the dock.'

Kingsmill Touched

Tiring of the lounge, they asked for a fire in a sitting-room upstairs, and sat there after supper, Kingsmill reading a slim volume which he had found between an old Bradshaw and an older Wisden. 'This is extraordinarily interesting,' he exclaimed after a time. 'It's an account by a Lady de Lancy of how she made her way to the field of Waterloo after the battle, and nursed her husband, one of Wellington's officers.' He read on, and having finished the wife's story of her husband's agonizing death put the book down, and looking sombrely at his friend said: 'Here we are, shovelled on to this bloody planet without any idea where we've come from, where we're going to, or who or even what we are.' This outburst over, he felt better, and handing the volume to Pearson said that, apart from its other merits, it was a very good piece of autobiographical writing, even if not in the style of Bernard Shaw's preface to *Immaturity*. 'By the way,' he continued, clearing his throat, 'I used the fact that you have just embarked on a life of Shaw in a manner which may jar on you. When you asked me to come on this holiday, I had no money due at the moment on the book I'm doing, and I need hardly tell you that I had no money due on any of my previous books. So I had to find some to keep my family going while I was away. After much reflection it occurred to me that as you were taking this trip to tone yourself up for your Shaw biography, a kind of connexion, however frail, had established itself between Shaw and me. Of course, I had to admit to myself that that article of mine in the *Fortnightly* the other day might rather weaken my value from Shaw's standpoint as the travelling companion of some one who would shortly be analysing the relations between Shaw, Harris and Wilde. But reflecting that it was fine points like this which bunkered the poor cat in the adage, I drew a deep breath and set off for London. On arriving I got Shaw's telephone number from William Gerhardi, and rang him up. I thought he would probably be in the country for the week-end, or at least that I should have to get past his secretary. So I was greatly relieved when I heard his voice. I said I wished to see him on a matter connected with Hesketh Pearson, and he asked me to come round in an hour.

'When I arrived at Whitehall Court a maid showed me into his room. He was sitting upright at his writing-table silhouetted against the window. Though I had other things to think of, there was something moving about the mixture of tenacity and solitude in the old man's erect bearing. Rising at once, he showed me to a chair with the shy courtesy I had noticed the two other times I met him. The conversation developed as follows —but I must just say that the first moving impression quickly vanished, and I saw from his alert eye that he smelt mischief in the air.

G. B. S. Well, and how is Hesketh? It is about him that you wished to see me?

Me: He's not very fit at present, and wants to go into the country. He's asked me to go with him, and I thought that as you're interested in Hesketh——

G. B. S.: I'm not interested in Hesketh. Hesketh's interested in me.

Me: I really can't go on with my preposterous errand unless you're willing to listen to me.

G. B. S.: Quite so, quite so.

Me: Hesketh's my host, and I can't ask him to support my family while I'm away. I have just published a book on D. H. Lawrence which has fizzled out, and I have no cash at the moment.

G. B. S.: T. E. finished D. H. Lawrence off. There's no interest in D. H. any more.

Me: So I have found. I wondered therefore if you would care to come to my assistance.

G. B. S.: But what about Sir Henry? He's still alive, isn't he?

Me: He's on a cruise, and in any case, apart from other complications, the travel business isn't what it was.

G. B. S.: That's a fine hotel your firm has up in Scotland. And there's that one at Hastings. I have stayed there myself.

Me: So have I.   None the less . . .

G. B. S.: I'm a poor man, too.   I've just had to
borrow two thousand from my wife.

Me: I'm so sorry.   (*Rising*).   In that case . . .

G. B. S.: Would a tenner be of any use?

Me (*Sinking back*): Certainly.   It's extremely good
of you.

'He stretched out his arm, took a cheque-book from
a drawer, and wrote out the cheque.   I rose, he gave me
the cheque and we shook hands.   As he accompanied
me to the door, he looked, I thought, a little bemused.
I was really touched, and was conscious of a very warm
feeling towards the old man, but was unable to find
words in which to express it.   Well, that's all, and I
hope you don't think it too outrageous.'

Pearson: Not at all.   But why didn't you touch him
for a hundred while you were about it?

Kingsmill: That might have put him in an awkward
position with his wife.

Pearson: It may interest you to know his views on
philanthropy, as expressed to me the other day.
He told me that he hated giving money away, hated
the person to whom he gave it quite as much as the
person to whom he gave it hated him, and was
frightened out of his life when some one stated
in public that he was generous, because at least
ten thousand begging letters arrived the following
week.

Kingsmill: Ah, well. . . .

Undenominational

On Monday, finding that there was no bus service which would get them to Chipping Campden and back in the day, they took the train to Gloucester, where they loitered in the Cathedral, Pearson for the most part sunk in comatose tranquillity, while Kingsmill read memorial inscriptions.

Meandering along, they came to St. Nicholas, an evangelical church which was obviously a centre of missionary enterprise. Affixed to a wall was a map of 'Gloucester people serving overseas'. At the moment there appeared to be no one in South America, but the needs of India, China, Australia, New Zealand and the East Coast of Africa were being attended to.

'"Miss C. Tippett, North China",' Kingsmill read out. 'It sounds forlorn and heroic. I doubt if any other country has ever supplied a parallel to the English spinster lady who with a Bible in one hand and a tea-caddy in the other penetrates to the wildest places of the earth as though visiting at the other end of a cathedral town. When I was living at Thonon I heard a very strange story from a woman evangelist there. As Thonon is on the south shore of Lake Geneva, I was surprised to find an English mission and mission house there, having always assumed that there was a tacit agreement among Europeans not to attempt to Christianize one another. Its origin was, in fact, accidental. In the sixties or seventies of the last century, the woman evangelist told me, two spinster ladies left England for missionary work in China. One of them had some trouble with her eyes, so they decided to visit Lausanne on the way, and see an oculist there. The oculist said China was out of the question, and advised the ladies to return to England. But learning that the opposite shore of the lake was in France, they took heart again, and crossing the eight or nine miles between Lausanne, Swiss and Protestant, and Thonon, French and Catholic, they settled there. It is a market town, with a fishing village by the lake. The two ladies started an undenominational mission, and soon became much beloved in the fishing village, where in a hundred ways and without charge they cared for the bodies of the inhabitants instead of, like the local priests, making them pay for the hypothetical salvation of their souls.

'The priests, concerned over their dwindling takings, denounced the English ladies as heretics, but of course if one calls oneself undenominational, and confines oneself strictly to succouring the needy, the most practised heresy-hunter is rather at a loss.

'Sharper measures seemed to be called for, and one of the priests, acting presumably on his own, resolved to make use of an old cannon, dating from the French Revolutionary wars, and at that time on exhibit outside the Town Hall. The Englishwomen lived in a villa on the table-land above the lake, at a short distance from the town. Unable to raise volunteers in Thonon itself to shift the cannon within range of the villa, the priest recruited four stalwarts from a neighbouring village, and under cover of night got the cannon into position. The priest's plan was to drop a cannon ball on to the double bed shared by the Englishwomen. He had learnt in what corner of the room the bed stood, and was therefore able to train the cannon on his target. But that very afternoon the Englishwomen had shifted the bed to the opposite corner of the room, one of them having told the other that she didn't know why, but she'd be happier if the bed were moved. So the cannon ball crashed on to the floor.

'The story got about in Thonon, where it was hailed as a miracle, immensely increasing the prestige of undenominational religion, and proportionately lowering the authority of the priests.'

Scenes One Would Like to Have Witnessed

They had sandwiches and drinks in the Bell Inn, where Fielding often stayed, presumably for nothing after the cordial praise he lavished on it in *Tom Jones*.

On the wall by the office there was a photograph of a bust of Fielding, and Pearson was greatly taken by it.

Pearson: What a delightful face! I'm awfully glad to see he was such a pleasant-looking fellow, for I have always regarded him with the admiration due to a perfect gentleman who is also a great artist—a unique phenomenon.

Kingsmill: I'm afraid the sculptor has idealized him. It's the late nineteenth century view of him— Saintsbury and Austin Dobson. There's only one contemporary portrait of him, and he is distinctly formidable in it, with a hooked nose and jutting jaw. He had to push his way through a very tough world—managing a theatre in the squalid days before Garrick refined the stage, and cleaning up the London gangsters in the last year of his life.

Pearson: There are few things I would rather have seen than Fielding on the bench.

Kingsmill: What are the few things?

Pearson: Shakespeare at a rehearsal of *Henry IV*, because I should have seen the greatest of poets speaking his verse in the way he wished it to be spoken, and the greatest of humorists trying to make the actor Pope understand that Falstaff was not merely a comic character. Next, Beethoven rehearsing one of his later symphonies, because I should have liked to catch the look on his face when something went wrong, and seen the expression in his eyes when everything went right. Last and least, Dickens reading scenes from his novels— a born actor playing all the parts in a show devised exclusively by himself.

Kingsmill: I'd have liked to see Shakespeare screaming at Burbage that only a fool like him could fail to grasp that *Timon of Athens* would be a more certain draw than *Hamlet.* And then I'd like to have seen him writing that line in *Lear* 'No, no, no, no, come, let's away to prison!'—the moment in all his life perhaps when he was most deeply moved. And for Beethoven, I'd choose him wandering about the fields in his last and greatest years, about the time when a kindly woman, seeing him on a bench with two or three peasants, sent out a glass of wine for the poor man who didn't seem quite right in his mind. And, for Johnson, the look on his face when after his paralytic stroke he wrote to Mrs.

Thrale, whom he was never to meet again: 'Let not all our endearments be forgotten, but let me have in this great distress your pity and your prayers.'

As to Dickens, I should have greatly enjoyed a meeting with Thackeray.

Pearson: Of course, Thackeray was much better worth meeting than Dickens. He was so much more human and charming. But what particular moment in his life appeals to you?

Kingsmill: Charles Brookfield breaking it to him that it would be better if he did not call again, as every one was beginning to talk.

Pearson: I quite agree. That's the moment I should choose, too.

Kingsmill: As a fashionable mid-Victorian preacher, Brookfield would know just the note to strike, and his wife being so beautiful and so conscious of her appeal, no doubt he had had some practice before striking it for Thackeray's benefit.

Pearson: 'It is good of you, William, to come so promptly in response to my note. My wife is resting, and in any case could hardly participate in what I have to say.

Kingsmill: 'I want, before I go any further, to assure you, not only in my name, but also in my wife's, how much your friendship has meant to both of us—to her no less than to me.

Pearson: 'But, my dear William, you, of all men, will agree with me that people are what they are, and that, try as we may, we cannot alter their natures.

Kingsmill: 'Where a great principle is at stake, nothing would be less pardonable than to take idle talk and uncharitable misinterpretation into account. But where personal happiness alone is concerned, I feel, and you, I know, will feel too, that sacrifices must be made where, if they are not made, an occasion for offence may be given to the weaker brethren.

Pearson: 'We have both of us received, each in his own way, a sacred charge. You with your pen, I in my pulpit, are alike trying to remind those who, by reason of their worldly advantages, are

peculiarly exposed to certain temptations, of that higher way from which it is so pitifully easy to wander.'

Kingsmill: At this point I'm afraid poor Thackeray would play straight into Brookfield's hands:
'You mean, Charles . . . you mean, that your home is no longer to be mine?'

Pearson: To which Brookfield, rising, would reply, with tears in his eyes and a catch in his voice:
'My dear friend . . .'

Kingsmill: And easing Thackeray into the hall, and helping him on with his coat, would, having opened the door, take his hand in both his own, saying: 'If we are not to meet again here, we shall, I doubt not, meet in a better place.'

At Stroud, on their way back, the train stopped some minutes in the station, and looking at the steep hills about them, the height of which seemed to be accentuated by the still lingering snow, Pearson said that people did not realize how high the Cotswold plateau was. On the South Downs one saw the weald and the sea below, but on the Cotswolds only a wide rolling plain. That was true, said Kingsmill. He had been quite unconscious of the descent from Cirencester to Gloucester, and yet it was clear they would have to rise to the level of the hills ahead of them, if they were to see Cirencester again. However, he presumed the train knew its own business.

Frank Harris

Two elderly citizens came into the lounge that evening, sat down, ordered drinks and opened their papers. After a while one of them, laying down his paper, said to the other:

'Nobody seems to be taking any more notice of China and Japan, eh?'

'That's so.'

'Too much going on here—Hitler, eh?'

'That's so.'

'Even war's bad enough, but this pogrom—pretty brutal, eh?'

'That's so.'

'We've always been able to live upsides with the Jews—
Disraeli Premier, eh?'

'That's so.'

They left, and some citizens of another kind came
in, settled themselves at the far end of the lounge, and
ordered drinks. The impression Pearson and Kingsmill
gradually formed was that they were observing a business
meeting between three local men and a Londoner, one
of the local men being probably on the town council.
Spread out on a table were specifications and plans,
and clearly a building deal was in progress.

Kingsmill: Our interest in their proceedings seems to
be rattling them a bit. This is the point on a
Shakespearean pilgrimage at which Frank Harris
would have woken up, and he wouldn't have
gone to sleep again until those chaps had either
let him in on the deal, or bought him off.

Pearson: It's rather hard that this should be the first
time on our trip we remember our old hero
Frankie.

Kingsmill: When we outgrow a youthful enthusiasm,
we forget all but its fatuity. 'The Man
Shakespeare and his Tragic Life Story'—that seems
overcharged now, but in our early twenties we
could do with being overcharged after being
undernourished so long.

Pearson: Frankie's Shakespeare was at any rate a
human being with parts and passions.

Kingsmill: 'It may be well for us to learn what
infinite virtue lay in that frail sensual singer.'

Pearson: It gives me quite a thrill to hear that again.

Kingsmill: I still remember reflecting that if that was

the way to being virtuous, I could be counted upon to try my hardest.

Pearson: I wonder if you made as big a nuisance of yourself over Frankie as I did. I reached my peak when I was the secretary of that Shakespearean Society. We used to hold an annual elocution competition, the prizes for which were presented by our President, Princess Marie Louise. The prizes were books, and on other occasions had been of all shapes and sizes. But on the occasion to which I refer the prizes were chosen by me, and the table in front of the Princess was loaded with two piles, those on the right of one size and shape, those on the left of another. The pile to the right largely consisted of Harris's *The Man Shakespeare*. These were for the male competitors. The pile to the left largely consisted of Harris's *The Women of Shakespeare*. These were for the female competitors.

After the prize-giving the Princess expressed some astonishment to Acton Bond over the sameness of the prizes, and he told me that I had placed him in an extremely invidious position. It had positively conveyed the impression that we were interested in the sale of that fellow Harris—a person who had no standing at all in the Shakespearean world.

Kingsmill: My peak was reached with a person who had a very high standing in the Shakespearean world—Sir Israel Gollancz.

Pearson: A vice-president of our Society.

Kingsmill: I was going in for the Shakespeare prize at Oxford in order to redeem my downfall in the Honour Schools, and a don at London University, who was coaching me, advised me to have a talk with Gollancz. Sir Israel gave me an appointment, and I went out to his house at Brondesbury. He was a quiet little man, stout, dark and subdued. Our talk, which lasted for about an hour, seemed to me to go swimmingly. I kept on pressing Harris's view that Shakespeare's own experiences, and especially his amorous ones, were reflected throughout his work, and in my enthusiasm failed altogether to perceive that this view was extremely repugnant to Gollancz. In fact I only, and then very dimly, realized what he was going through when he muttered that perhaps there was some personal emotion in *Othello*. Here, possibly, in the feelings of an elderly man married to a much younger woman, there might be a reflection of some situation which Shakespeare had taken from real life.

Still brimming with enthusiasm, and radiating goodwill towards my host, I rose, and he accompanied me to the front door. We shook hands, and there was a slight pause. I felt he had something to say. He had. 'Young man, what you need is a very good kicking.' The door closed.

Pearson: Did you get that Shakespeare prize?
Kingsmill: No.

Spotlight

On Tuesday, January 31, the travellers returned to London. In the train they discussed what other places they would have to visit later on, in order to complete their material for *Falstaff's Ghost*, and Kingsmill reminded Pearson that they must deal with Shakespeare from the actor's standpoint.

Pearson: In other words I must deal with it.

Kingsmill: That was in my mind. It only means talking about yourself. Treat me, within limits, as Othello treated Desdemona. Run it over even from your boyish days. I've had most of it 'in parcels'. Let me now have it all in a sack.

Pearson: I went on the stage in 1911, having already witnessed the old actor-manager system in its Indian summer. Its strong point was that it produced great actors, such as Shakespeare wrote for. Its weak point was that it blotted out everything in Shakespeare which interfered with the star part. Beerbohm Tree, for example, when he produced *Antony and Cleopatra*, not only cut down the play by a third so as to allow for the changing of elaborate sets of scenery, but also transposed some scenes, and ran others together, all with the sole object of concentrating everything on himself. He had to allow Cleopatra, in view of the part she played in Antony's life, to share his limelight, but Enobarbus, the next most important part, was quite another matter. That part was played by a really superb actor, Lyn Harding . . .

Kingsmill: I remember him well, though I only saw him once, thirty years ago at Oxford in *The Speckled Band*. I can still see him beetling terrifically over Holmes.

Pearson: I was present at the fiftieth night of Tree's show and at the end the whole house rose at Harding when he appeared with the others before the curtain, and that although an entire act, crammed with Tree and Cleopatra, had intervened since Enobarbus's last appearance. The audience went on shouting, and Tree went on appearing, taking all the calls for Harding. And when the entire theatre united in a single roar of HARDING, the lights went up and the National Anthem was played.

There you have the actor-manager system at its worst, but as I said it had at any rate the virtue of producing great actors, if only in the leading parts. The modern method, though it sticks to the text, is to speak great poetry as if it were suburban small talk.

Kingsmill: Hamlet, prince of Denmark Hill. What the moderns don't realize is that Shakespeare's language was not the ordinary language of his day. It was poetry to the Elizabethans, so why should it be Peckham to us?

Pearson: Another drawback to the actor-manager system was the long run. Irving's *Much Ado* and Tree's *Henry VIII* each ran about a year. When actors have to repeat the same words night after night, some of the spontaneity oozes away by the time the hundredth performance is reached. Should you fail to grasp this, a single example will make it plain. A year or two after the last war I was playing the guardian of the two children in *The Blue Lagoon* at the Prince of Wales's Theatre, and at the end of six months had become completely automatic. At one point I had to narrate the sad story of the two little blighters to another character. My words were—'Little Emmeline's father, captain, died before she was born. Her mother died in giving her birth.' But one evening the automatic process went wrong, and I opened as follows: 'Little Emmeline's mother, captain, died before she was born.' Interpreting the agonized convulsion on the captain's face as due to some humorous recollection, very out of place at the moment, and wishing to steady him, I drove the next point home with all the emphasis at my command: '*Her father died in giving her birth.*' The house rocked for at least two minutes, and the captain, turning his back on the audience, shook from bow to stern. Fortunately at this point a storm arose and the ship went down, with the captain on board.

'*AND Heavenly Rosalind!*'

At Paddington, before parting, they went into the buffet. They felt depressed: London once more after Cirencester and Fairford, but they consoled themselves with the prospect of resuming their pilgrimage in due course.

Pearson: And the first place we'll make for is Salisbury.

Kingsmill: Salisbury?

Pearson: Yes, Wilton, where Shakespeare performed in *As You Like It* before James I and his court.

Kingsmill: I didn't know that.

Pearson: Cory, the poet of *Heraclitus*, was staying at Wilton in the sixties of last century, and was told by his hostess that the family had a letter written in 1604 by the Countess of Pembroke to her son, who was with James at Salisbury. In it she asked her son to bring the king over to a performance of *As You*, and added 'We have the man Shakespeare with us.'

Kingsmill: What mixed feelings that sentence would have given Shakespeare, if he had seen it! 1604, too, just after struggling through the Hamlet-Troilus morass.

Pearson: And now compelled to return to the *As You* mood, play the obsequious old Adam, and register doddering rapture over the innocent fun of Rosalind and Orlando.

Kingsmill: Alias Cressida and Dismedes, as they would appear to his disillusioned eye. One can see him, after he had been summoned by the countess to be patronized by the king, alone in his bedroom. King, court and Rosalind, wealth, women and Wilton—all equally horrible to him.

Pearson began to declaim:

'Thus must I from the smoke into the smother,
From tyrant duke unto a tyrant brother.'

A maniac grin overspread his face, and with fixed eyes and through clenched teeth he screamed:
'AND *heavenly* Rosalind!'
A shattered waitress desparately clutched her tray.

An Optimistic Forecast

As they were unable to find a publisher to replace Hamish Hamilton, they were compelled to lay Falstaff's ghost for the time being, Pearson retiring to Chipperfield to write his life of Shaw, and Kingsmill, at Hastings, spending the spring and summer on a novel, *The Fall*. Early in September, a few days after the declaration of war, they met again, in Pearson's flat at 144 Goldhurst Terrace, N.W.6.

Pearson and his wife were having tea in the garden,

and Mrs. Pearson having expressed some gloomy forebodings about the war, Kingsmill assured her that there was no reason for despondency. Taxed with outrageous optimism, he replied that he was optimistic about everything he could not control, and as he could control practically nothing, he was optimistic about practically everything. That, said Mrs. Pearson, was all very well for him, especially as he lived in Hastings, but would not be of much use to her when the Germans started dropping bombs on London.

Kingsmill: I see that. But, taking a broad view, I am convinced that this war won't last half the time of the last one, and that there won't be anything like as much bloodshed. Spain has just lost two million men because she wasn't in the last war, and so had a lot of superfluous energy to let off. I was in Germany in 1913, and every one was bursting for war—toy Zeppelins in every shop window. I should say that the German of 1913 weighed, on an average, two stones more than the German of to-day. He had to fight or burst. The German of to-day, after all he has gone through in the last twenty-five years, wants nothing but a quiet life. Hitler doesn't symbolize pugnacity, but resentment and despair. He may have whipped up the youth of the country, but you can't fight a long war with nothing behind you but the bloodlust of perverted boy scouts.

Mrs. Pearson: You really think it'll only last two years?

Kingsmill: If that.

Mrs. Pearson: I'll remind you of this in two years' time.

Kingsmill: Do, if I turn out to be right. Otherwise it would be kinder to say nothing.

Pearson: Personally, I have not the slightest doubt that we shall smash the Germans, just as we smashed Napoleon and Louis XIV and Philip of Spain and . . .

Mrs. Pearson: Oh, you two! You talk just like Kipling.

Pearson and *Kingsmill:* Kipling!

The Falls

After a brief pause Pearson asked Kingsmill to explain if he could why he had returned to fiction from biography. 'You have, I gathered from an understandably reticent reference in one of your letters, been writing a novel.'

Kingsmill: A few weeks after our Shakespearean pilgrimage, my brother Brian fell from a bus. He was taken to a hospital about a mile from where I live, and I went along to see him. He was unconscious, and looked very impressive, breathing heavily with a stern look on his face, as though the rest of us had been tried and found wanting. During the next few days, as he slowly recovered consciousness, his wanderings—'reason and impertinency mix'd'—gradually crystallized a number of feelings and thoughts in my mind—but I don't quite see why I should extenuate my novel in the spirit of a girl explaining her seduction to her father confessor, especially as your face gives little promise of absolution.

Pearson: You have my attention.

Kingsmill: Which I will not weary further, except with a point illustrative of the Victorian attitude on these occasions. The aunts, uncles and so forth who wrote to me for news of Brian all insisted what a blow it would be to his father, when the news reached him—he was on a cruise at the time. So I asked them to bear in mind that Brian had fallen on his head, not on his father's, after which their interest died away.

A few weeks ago, when my novel was nearly over, and its hero had just emerged from hospital, I was rung up from St. Bartholomew's, and told that my brother Brian was there. He had had a fall, and would I come up? Repressing an impulse to tell St. Bartholomew's that there was no point in my coming up, as I had just completed my hospital scenes, I went to London. Brian has a genius for the unexpected. I thought I should find him stern, white and unconscious, but as I entered his bedroom he was smiling broadly, very red in the face, his nose twice its usual size, one of his eyes blackened, and a strip of plaster about five inches long running down his bald crown, with another crossing it at right angles. He was not too bad, he said. It was just an after-effect of his accident, a momentary loss of consciousness going down the steps of Cannon Street Station.

After I left him, I came along to this part of the world, to recover a manuscript Brian thought he might have left with a friend who lives near here. I hoped you might be at home, but there was no answer when I rang up.

Pearson: No, I've been at Chipperfield with very few breaks. Life for me, since we last met, has been almost undiluted Shaw. You, on the other hand, apart from your round of hospitals, appear to have been in Ireland, if a post card you sent me from Killarney is any clue.

Kingsmill: I was there at the end of April. I took my mother to Cork, where a sister of hers lives, and never having seen Killarney went on there for a day or two.

Pearson: Did it come up to your expectations?

Ireland

Kingsmill: It was very beautiful, but I wasn't in the mood to enjoy it. I used to love Ireland, but on this visit, from the moment I saw its sad fields and straggling trees from the deck of the ship, I felt depressed. Nothing seemed solid. As we steamed up to the docks, Cork looked unreal, as though the genuine Cork were being held in reserve, and this shabby imitation had been dumped down over night. The melancholia in the eyes of the men hanging round the docks was like something seen in a dream. It didn't seem to spring from anything so prosaic as want of cash. Of course I met more cheerful people later on, but the general impression I came away with was that Ireland lacks something of which we have just enough, and the Germans far too much—earthiness, contact with this life, or whatever you like to call it. Hence their fascination in their livelier moments. A lack of ballast has its advantages, and I shall never forget a dance I saw at Killarney. It was the usual Saturday night hop for the inhabitants of the place, all the current dance tunes, but the speed and the wild grace of the dancers, and the ardour of the violinist, a beautiful girl—well, in comparison any English dance hall might be a parade of dyspeptic tortoises working away under doctor's orders.

If I hadn't felt depressed from the moment I sighted land, I should be inclined to attribute my jaundiced feeling to an experience I had on my first day. My mother's father was a Church of Ireland parson, and I thought it would be pleasant to revisit the place where he used to live. Walking through the town, which had all the decay but none of the liveliness I remembered from my early years, I passed the rectory and went on towards Hillside, a house about three miles from the town, where a girl had lived with whom I was in love in my teens. Hillside was high above the surrounding country, with a distant view of the sea, and the beauty of the landscape and the blissful pain of adoring the unresponsive Cecily formed a whole which I had never altogether forgotten.

Although I looked forward to seeing the place again, I had more solid misgivings than the usual fear of failing to revive a dead emotion. I knew that Cecily's elder sister, Gwendolen, had married the son of the local washerwoman, that Cecily and her mother had retreated to England, and that Hillside itself had been accidentally set on fire by one of Gwendolen's children and almost entirely consumed. That was fifteen years ago, but Gwendolen, according to a vague rumour, was still living at Hillside, though her husband was long since dead.

She had married him at the close of the Great War, when she was thirty-five or six, and he nineteen. Gwendolen was versatile, she could do many things quite well, and during the war she had grown crops on the estate, Connor, her future husband, acting as her foreman. As their intimacy grew, she became increasingly unpunctual for meals, striding in late to dinner in heavy boots caked with mud, her mother, a formal handsome Englishwoman, sitting at the head of the table with an unmoved expression, Cecily on her left, also expressionless, and on her right her eldest daughter, who at nearly forty had the mind of a child of three or four.

One evening, when Gwendolen was in the loft above the stables, Connor came up the ladder with a lantern in his hand, and looking at her exclaimed: 'By God, Miss Gwendolen, I wish I was a gentleman.' 'You are a man, Connor,' she replied, and he took her in his arms. A few weeks later her mother and sisters left for England.

As I walked along I felt more and more depressed, and when I turned off the main road at the entrance to Hillside a pang of homesickness overcame me at the sight of a stunted pylon, unworthy of the

Sussex landscape, but a lively and attractive object in the melancholy scene about me.

The road up through the wood was grass-grown, and four shabby sheep were walking down it with a casual air which provoked me. I passed them coldly, and coming into the open saw the house on the slope above me. It was roofless, with blackened walls, and as I drew nearer I could see grass and young saplings in the rooms on the ground floor. Repressing an impulse to turn back, I walked past the front door, and going round to the side, where the kitchen quarters were still standing, I knocked, and getting no answer knocked again. There was a shuffling within, and the door opened. In her youth Gwendolen had been, though not beautiful, very striking, with black eyes, long silky black hair, and a cream pale complexion. She was toothless now, her cheeks were rough and coarse, her hair dusty and straggling and her clothes tattered, shapeless and thrown on anyhow. One thing only remained, her self-possession, based on an innate feeling of superiority to the rest of mankind.

'Why, it's Hugh!' she exclaimed. 'Come in!' She paused, and then in her old assured tone added: 'You are a Bohemian, and won't mind a little disorder.'

I followed her through the kitchen into a kind of scullery, lit by two small windows. There was a bed—no sheets, but some blankets thrown back as though she had just got out, as I suppose she had, though it was past two.

'Well,' she said, 'where have you sprung from ?

Sit down.' We sat down opposite one another, and picking up some twigs and fragments of newspaper she lit a fire on an unswept hearth. 'I am afraid,' she said, 'that I have nothing much to offer you. This is my lunch.' She pointed to a packet of Ryvita biscuits. I said I had lunched already, so she poured some lime juice into a tumbler, added water from an earthenware jug, and handed me the tumbler, filling another for herself.

At first we talked about our times together in Switzerland. She was perfectly sane about that distant period, and narrated in detail a climb she had made from Saas Fee, alone and by night. The mountain was one which most people took two days over, with a guide to look after them. It was an extraordinary feat, and you can get a good deal of her character from it.

The fire went out every few minutes, and she would throw on some more twigs and bits of paper and put a match to them. Presently I heard something moving about in the kitchen. She had just begun to tell me about her marriage, her manner had changed a little, becoming more restless, and I must have been feeling the strain, for the sound next door was getting on my nerves. 'That cat!' she said, rather irritably; and with an air of taking up a challenge the cat walked in, and asked curtly for milk, I put it like that because that was exactly the effect her mewing made on me. 'Here you are,' said Gwendolen, pouring some milk into a saucer. Lapping it up, the cat looked sharply at Gwendolen, and rapped out: 'Is that all you've got for me, you old devil?'

'Very well, then. Here's some more.' 'I should hope so.'

This interchange over, Gwendolen resumed the story of her marriage. The ordinary kind of marriage, she said, had never attracted her. When she was a girl she had made up her mind that if she married at all, it must be either a prince or a peasant. In her old allusive way she hinted vaguely at a morganatic marriage, which would have taken place but for insuperable obstacles.

'Connor was a perfect lover,' she went on.

'We were made for one another. But he never called me "Gwendolen". It was always "my love", and I always called him "Connor". He never entered the drawing-room. Tea was served to me there by his mother, but he and his mother had their meals in the kitchen.'

She told me about the fire, and in an increasingly disconnected way about the later years of poverty and growing dissensions with her husband. She wanted the children educated as Protestants, but he would not have this, and there was a court case. 'I told them in court that I had come straight from

10 Downing Street. I spoke of my friend Mrs. Asquith. You can imagine the effect on bumpkins like them.' She stared at me triumphantly.

'After that I was all alone here. The children come to see me sometimes, but I can't do anything for them at present. They are very distinguished-looking, and later I'll be able to help them. I'm still top dog—but it's very annoying to be top dog with nothing to be top dog on.' She looked across at me with a puzzled expression, then resumed:

'I was warned he meant to murder me, but I wasn't afraid of him. One day when I came in, he was here, sitting on the kitchen table. I knew he was dying when I saw him. "I've come back," he said. "We were made for each other. I couldn't keep away any longer." But his mother took him. I went down to her house, and she came out and said: "You've had him all these years, but I have him now, and I'm going to keep him. He never wants to see you again." I promised that if he told me with his own lips he didn't want me any more, I'd never trouble him again, and she let me in. He was in bed, and I asked him if what his mother said was true. He said "Leave me". I never saw him again.'

We talked of other things, and when I rose she said she would come part of the way with me. As we went along, she told me she had developed certain powers, and had been in some degree responsible for the settlement at Munich. She could also foretell financial changes by the clouds. 'I don't mean my own affairs. I mean the general situation. That dark cloud over there is unfavour-able, but that one with the light on it indicates an improvement.'

I became conscious of a reluctance to look at her, and this was succeeded by an illusion that she was young again, with a clear pale face. I half knew it was an illusion, and to preserve it looked straight ahead, while she went on talking about her powers. But suddenly, in an ordinary voice, she said: 'Well, I have told you everything, but you needn't believe it, for it's all too bad.'

We parted about half a mile from the town. She trailed back up the road in her rusty tattered clothes, like an old gipsy woman, and I watched her for some time, but she did not look back, and had probably already forgotten my existence.

Pearson: A strange story, but Ireland is a very strange country. Before 1914 I spent some of my happiest holidays at my brother's place in County Limerick and also in Clare. There is a freedom from con-vention about the Irish which I found extremely refreshing. What English son of toil would call aloud to an English countess at a point-to-point meeting 'Och, your ladyship! May yer drawers never grow tighter on ye!' And what English countess would accept such a salutation in a friendly spirit? I witnessed the salutation, and felt that the Irish could teach us a lesson in democracy.

But they are also a very odd people. Most of their lunatics seem to be at large. I knew of one descendant of an ancient house whose whim it was to entertain fifty people to dinner every night; and every night the table was laid for fifty guests;

and every night, dressed in the fashion of the late eighteenth century, he entered the dining-room beneath the crossed swords of a dozen retainers, bowed gravely to the fifty empty seats, took his place at the head of the table, and went solemnly through the courses, occasionally dropping a courteous remark to the chair on his right or left. At the conclusion of the meal he stood up, the swords of his retainers flashed to the salute, and he toasted the King 'over the water'. A little

later he rose, politely excused himself, left the fifty no-men over their port, and passed out beneath crossed swords.

Once I lunched with a family near Kilmallock. I was vaguely conscious that our host seemed rather abstracted, and wondered why his son and another fellow should be placed on his immediate right and left when several women were present. But I did not pay much attention to him until I heard a snarl, and, glancing in his direction, saw that he was straining to get at something his hands could not reach. Then I noticed that he was wearing metal bracelets, which were attached to thin steel chains. My surprise was so great that I must have stopped eating, for the lady to whom I was talking asked me whether I had lost my appetite. I could not conceal from her that I was interested in the proceedings at the head of the table. She told me in a matter-of-fact voice that I need not feel anxious, as our host was quite safe. 'Safe?' I echoed. 'Yes,' she replied; 'he is chained to the table.' 'But why?' 'Oh, don't you know? He has homicidal tendencies, and the knives have to be kept out of his reach.'

That sort of thing appeared to be fairly common among the better-class Irish families, and by the time I had spent several holidays in the district I could regard the strange behaviour of Mr. Green as a normal occurrence.

Mr. Green lived in a large mansion a few miles from the city of Limerick. Some time in the eighteen-eighties he decided to go to bed. He must have been rather tired, for he had hardly been in bed a month before he made up his mind to stay there. The years went by; Queen Victoria celebrated her golden and diamond jubilees, died and was succeeded by Edward VII; still Mr. Green remained in bed, unaffected by these circumstances, and with no intention of getting up again.

One summer day, about twenty years after his rest-cure had commenced, two young women, enjoying a holiday with their camera in southern Ireland, were much taken by the appearance of his mansion. They got off their bicycles, and inspected the apparently deserted building from the other side of the crumbling walls. It looked extremely picturesque, almost hidden by creepers, and the weeds made the gravel drive indistinguishable from the grass-grown flower beds. It was easy to penetrate the wall, for the stones fell away when pushed, and soon they were setting up their camera before the semi-ruined house. But Mr. Green, whose bed on the first floor commanded the front lawn, viewed the intrusion of these

photo-fiends with suspicion. The women had just got their camera into position on its tripod, and were about to take their first picture of the peaceful old place, when to their alarm a series of sounds came from the neighbourhood of the porch. After some rattling and screeching the door flew open, and their alarm changed to horror as an old gentleman, with a bushy grey beard reaching to his waist, came bounding towards them, dressed in a nightshirt and brandishing a carving knife.

As they hared down the road on their bicycles,

they heard Rip Van Winkle slashing their camera to bits.

Kingsmill: Did he go back to bed afterwards?

Pearson: Presumably.

Dickens Encourages His Children to See Their Mother

Pearson returned to Chipperfield to work on his life of Shaw, which he continued at Ludlow, and finished, for the time being, in London, during the winter. Kingsmill meanwhile put together a portrait of Johnson from contemporary sources other than Boswell, and rashly entered upon a survey in one volume of the characters and careers of Elizabeth, Cromwell, Napoleon, Lincoln and Lenin.

The war continuing its peaceful course, Pearson and Kingsmill wondered if it might be possible to resume their Shakespearean pilgrimage, and in the middle of February, 1940, they approached another publisher, who in a few days wrote and thanked them for their kindness in putting such an interesting idea before him . . . very careful thought . . . unfortunately could not, at the present moment . . . later date, perhaps.

Another two months passed, and Kingsmill, wearying of his dictators, came to town to celebrate Shakespeare's birthday with Pearson. They finished up in the long bar at Victoria Station, where the sight of a stout sorrowful woman drinking beer reminded Kingsmill of Mrs.

Charles Dickens, and he asked his friend if he had seen a book by Gladys Storey on Dickens and his daughter, Kate Perugini. Pearson replied that he had read it in the previous autumn, and that it dotted the i's and crossed the t's of everything Kingsmill had implied in his book on Dickens.

Kingsmill: When, in 1934, I drew some obvious inferences after reading Thomas Wright's account of Dickens's affair with Ellen Ternan, one paper termed me a Freudian dabbling in offal and garbage. By 1939 Time, the healer, had softened the shock, and the same paper, reviewing Miss Storey, referred to Dickens as revealing a smug insensitiveness to his wife's feelings almost as outrageous as one of his own lampoons.

Pearson: I must say the new Dickens is far more amusing than the old one to which the Chestertonian diehards still feverishly cling. When I was reading Kate Perugini's memories of home life in the Dickens household, after Mrs. Dickens had been shot out on her left ear, I formed a very vivid picture of the kind of encouragement Dickens gave his children to continue seeing their mother. No doubt they were so unfeeling as to want to see her, and the moment must have come when Dickens, sensing discontent in the fo'c'sle, summoned them to his cabin. I see them filing in, their ages ranging from four to eighteen, and Dickens snapping: 'Sit down. You, there . . . you, there. . . . Don't fidget and don't crowd!

Kingsmill: 'It is now three months since your mother has taken up a separate domicile. The reasons for this step are generally within your knowledge. I have nothing to say about them, here and now, and my wish that you should keep silent on this sacred subject is wholly known to you.

Pearson: 'This morning I am concerned solely with the fit relation between you and your mother (don't fidget!). It would be altogether unnatural, and utterly removed from any desire which one such as I could feel or conceive, that any of you children should be deprived by others, or should, under a mistaken apprehension of my will and wishes, deprive yourselves of any imaginable comfort, or form or shape of innocent happiness, to which you are entitled by the accepted usages of civilized life. (Blow your nose!)

Kingsmill: 'I will not have it said that I have by so much as the lifting of a finger, or the least hinting of displeasure, ever, either directly or indirectly, insinuated or interposed the slightest barrier between you and your mother. (Don't suck your thumb!) No one of you shall to the furthest limit of your lives have it in your power to reproach me with darkening your happiness by the shadow of whatever secret sorrow falls on me, and will continue to fall.

Pearson: 'You have therefore my unconditional approval of any and all visits which each or any of you may now or hereafter feel desirous of making to your mother. (Don't shuffle your feet!) And do not be deterred by any thought of the agony which such conduct on your part must cause to throb in the mind which other conduct would allow, in time and in part, to heal.

Kingsmill: 'Nor would I have your decision in this

matter to be influenced by such welling up of gratitude as I am surely entitled to assume as existing among even the youngest and most un-thinking of you for those advantages of education and position and name which he who now speaks to you knew nothing of in his own poor early years. No more of that!

Pearson: 'If there be among you any who, weighing each word I have to-day uttered, should neverthe-less decide to visit your mother, rest assured that,

God helping me, and my strength and sanity continuing, I shall not in the smallest particular discriminate between them and those—God bless them!—who have weighed with a different measure, and reached a different result.'

An Interchange With Charles Laughton

Pearson accompanied Kingsmill to the train. There being still some minutes to run, he asked Kingsmill whether he had seen it reported that Charles Laughton had refused to appear as Dr. Johnson in a film, on the ground that Johnson 'never did anything but sit and make cruel remarks about other people'.

Kingsmill: Small beer to Laughton after Henry VIII, and the raping and murdering squire in *Jamaica Inn*.

Pearson: I once asked him why he hadn't played Falstaff. 'I dislike the type,' he answered. 'I've seen too many Falstaffs in a hotel where I used to live.' To this I naturally replied: 'I'd rather live in that hotel than anywhere else on earth. Where is it? If you can guarantee *one* Falstaff, I'll book a permanent room there.'

Kingsmill: What interests me is how the hotel-keeper remained solvent, with a mob of Falstaffs parked on him.

The train beginning to move, Pearson moved with it, ejaculating: 'All the same, Laughton gave an absolutely first-rate performance of Angelo in *Measure for Measure*. Like Kean, and unlike Garrick, he's the kind of actor who excels in portraying one type of character.'

'One type of *what*?' shouted Kingsmill to his receding friend.

'Character, curse you!' panted Pearson.

The French

In May, Pearson, who could no longer contain himself
on the subject of Shakespeare, withdrew to Washington
in Sussex, and set to on a biography of the poet. Meanwhile Kingsmill was grappling with his dictators, while
the Dutch, Belgians, French and English were failing to
grapple with theirs. At the beginning of the war he
had written to a number of schools, offering his services
as an English master, but as the months passed the hope
that his services might be required had faded out.
Then, in the general dissolution of everything during
the second half of May, the Maginot Line passed and
the fabric of France cracking, the Headmaster of Marlborough sent Kingsmill a telegram, asking him if he
could fill a gap for a fortnight. Kingsmill went, found
Marlborough almost as pleasant to work in as to
stroll through, and was asked to stay on for another
term.

In August Pearson was back at Chipperfield, and Kingsmill came up to London for a time to be near the British
Museum for his book on dictators. Pearson lent him
his flat, and occasionally looked in on him there.

'Well, Hesketh,' said Kingsmill, at their first meeting,
'a lot has happened since we last saw each other. The
French have certainly borne out my forecast that nations
who lost millions in the last war would not be prepared
to lose millions more in this.'

Pearson: One can't generalize from the French.
They only lost millions in the last war because
we were jollying them along. I've never under-

stood why the French have a great reputation as a military nation. Is it because Hilaire Belloc was once in the French army? I never think of the English as a military nation, yet we've thrashed the French whenever we've been up against them. True, they once got the better of us when they were led by a woman, but that was merely because Joan of Arc had never opened a book on military strategy. Apart from her, we flogged them under the Black Prince and Henry V; we made circles round them under Marlborough; Clive drove them out of India, Wolfe beat them out of Canada; one English general, named Sidney Smith, commanding a bunch of tommies at Acre, flung back Napoleon's Grand Army; another, Sir John Moore, upset his plans in Spain, where Wellington smashed all his leading marshals, and finished up by giving him an almighty hiding at Waterloo. Until the English got busy on Boney, he had chiefly been matched against Austrians, Italians, Russians, Poles, Mamelukes, and, of course, Frenchmen, and the story of his exploits should be entitled Money for Jam. We saved the French armies again and again in the 1914–18 scrap, and if they hadn't folded up in June with a rapidity amazing even for them, we'd have saved them yet again. They really ought to content themselves with being the world's best chefs. It's a reputation to be proud of. Every civilized being has a keener relish for a well-cooked omelette than for a well-fought battle.

Kingsmill: I suppose a Frenchman would reply that even Napoleon could not go on for ever beating the whole world, that the Marlborough wars ended more or less in a stalemate, and that the skirmishes at Crecy, Poitiers and Agincourt were purely temporary successes. Joan of Arc has been very useful to us. Although we roasted her alive, we have managed to convey the impression that we vacated France rather than lift our hand against a woman save in kindness. Actually the Hundred Years War ended, long after Joan of Arc's death, in the English being thrown out of France by French armies commanded by French males.

Pearson: I forgot I was addressing a schoolmaster.

Kingsmill: One picks up quite a lot as history master to the Lower Fourth. Among other things I have discovered that every nation has a totalitarian phase as soon as it becomes unified. We were unified under Edward III, and promptly fell upon France with the ferocity of a nation which has just become conscious of its existence. Spain was unified under Ferdinand and Isabella, and was the pest of the sixteenth century. France was unified under Richelieu, and broke loose under Louis XIV, with a final spasm under Napoleon. Germany was unified by Bismarck, and is nearing the end of her run. Italy was unified under Cavour, and has been trying to get off the mark ever since.

In my opinion, when the Germans have lost this war, they ought to be pretty well over their totalitarian phase. They may break out again, but I doubt it, for I think Hitler is to Bismarck what Napoleon was to Louis XIV, and that

Germany will be as exhausted after Hitler as France after Napoleon.

Pearson: What about Napoleon III?

Kingsmill: If Hitler the Second is as footling as Napoleon the Third, Germany's number will indeed be up. I could wish the last half of this century nothing better than a Fourth Reich on the level of the Second Empire.

Hampstead Heath and Regent's Park

A few days later Pearson came in from Chipperfield again, and he and Kingsmill went for a walk in Regent's Park.

Kingsmill: London is very peaceful at present. I have been up to Hampstead Heath several times. Occasionally a homing aeroplane zooms mildly towards Hendon, but there is little to remind one of the present struggle, or indeed of any struggle at all. Looking down at the city, and across at St. Paul's, one has a feeling as though the fight for existence among the poor, and for wealth and position among the others, were suspended. One might almost be in another world. Here the illusion is not quite so strong. That balloon station impairs it a little.

Pearson: It looks peaceful enough to me.

Kingsmill: Still, I suppose it's quite a strenuous job. It occurred to me the other day, when I was passing those chaps, that it must be rather annoying for them to feel that any casual passer-by, a child of four or a crone of ninety, was, for the time being, as much in the front line as themselves.

Pearson: And the annoyance doesn't stop there. In the cold spell last January I was passing this particular balloon unit. Two men were working on the lorry, while three kids, the oldest not above

ten, were improving the unshining hour by pelting them with snowballs. As I came up, one of the barragers shouted angrily at the kids: 'Clear off! What the devil do you think you're doing? We aren't here for fun.' Instantly the kid of ten, a girl, retorted: 'But we are.' The last I saw of them, the kids were being chased by one of the men. Having observed the face of the little girl, I feel sure the party returned.

H. G. Wells

Continuing their walk they passed Hanover Terrace. Pearson pointed to a house.

Pearson: Wells lives there. I went to see him exactly a year ago, when I was working on Shaw. He hadn't much to say about Shaw, beyond expressing a real liking for him, and the talk drifted to other matters. One of his sons was with him, and over tea Wells and I had a brief spar on the subject of biography. It began with his saying that people thought they were thoroughly educated because they had been to a public school or university— 'D'you think *you* can teach us anything?' was their attitude to him, said H. G. From the bootblack to the master of the college, he went on, they were just as annoyed when accused of being uneducated as the poor were annoyed when accused of being dirty, gross or inefficient. 'Yet what on earth is the use of an Oxford or Cambridge education?' he ended.

'Well, it produces our bishops,' I said.

'Is that a justification?'

'Yes. They hand us at least one good laugh a day.'

'Is that their object in life?'

'I can't think of any other.'

At this point Wells's son chipped in, telling us that a leading Bishop had once declared he would like to make a bonfire of all the contraceptives in the world, and dance round it.

'Do you still question the value of a varsity education?' I asked Wells.

He did not seem much amused, and a little later exclaimed: 'Why do people live in the past?'

'Because the past, which we know, is more interesting than the future, which we don't know?' I replied.

'Isn't the present good enough for you?'

'Yes, quite. But one of its principal charms is that it enshrines the past.'

'What's the use of biography, anyway?'

'What's the use of history, come to that?'

'History is a record of mistakes. It teaches people what to avoid.'

'Biography is a record of life. It shows people how to live.'

'I give it up,' said Wells, with a weary laugh.

'I should,' said I.

Kingsmill: I hope you parted amiably.

Pearson: Oh, quite. This little brush apart, he was really delightful, and offered to help me in any way he could. If I hadn't felt he'd heard it too often from the critics, I'd have told him how much pleasure his *Polly* and *Kipps* had given me. There was something very appealing about his sad humorous eyes.

Kingsmill: I paid him a visit seven years ago. He had been reading my book on Frank Harris, and some of my parodies, and he told a friend of mine, Zilliacus, that he'd like to meet me. So I wrote to him, and he wrote back asking me to come to tea, and adding 'You're ALL RIGHT'.

He must be very much a man of moods, for in

his autobiography, which came out a month or two later, I found unmistakable evidence that my parodies had annoyed him—at least the Johnson one, with those remarks about him which I put into Johnson's mouth. In the autobiography he referred to a modern trick of criticizing brilliant future-piercing thinkers through the mouth of some fusty old windbag, like Johnson. I forget the exact words, but that was the gist. Also, in recounting his first affair, he borrowed my name for the girl. It was a quick casual encounter, and he was at no pains at all to put 'Ethel Kingsmill', as he called her, in an attractive, to say nothing of a romantic, light. She was just the trivial kind of person one would expect a Kingsmill to be.

Seven years ago he was living in Chiltern Court. He kept me waiting some time, and looked very sleepy when he came in. I had probably interrupted an afternoon doze, but he took it well, and soon became quite animated.

From something he said about G. K.'s Weekly, in which my brother Arnold had recently been going for him, I inferred that he thought I was a Catholic, so I explained that I was not a member of any church.

'Then you're an outcast like me,' he said, and looked so forlorn that I felt inclined to suggest that we should pool our resources and face the world together. His mood altogether was rather wistful. He spoke with much affection of Arnold Bennett, and seemed to miss him greatly, and he spoke with sympathy even of Frankie, and I thought it was on his conscience he hadn't seen more of him when he was dying on the Riviera. 'But,' he said, 'I could never manage Harris in conversation. Shaw could, but he was too much for me.' And again he looked forlorn, weighed down by the burden of things.

The talk was warming up when the maid came in and announced some one.

'It's that young chap,' said Wells irritably. 'He was here this morning. I'll have to see him. Very well, show him in.'

A youth of nineteen or so entered, with an excited anticipatory expression, as though great things were in store for him.

He was, as I learnt in the next few minutes with some additional information when we went away together, a Scot who had left Glasgow for Manchester, where he had a job in a draper's shop. He had written to Wells about one of his books, Wells replied, he wrote again, and Wells suggested that, if he were ever in London, he should look in for a talk. The youth—Fraser was his name—had at once thrown up his job, arriving in London the previous evening, with the assistance of several motorists, whom he held up on the way. That morning he had called on Wells, and met him in the passage outside his flat.

'Does Mr. Wells live on this floor?' he asked.

'Second door on the right,' Wells replied.

'But—but you *are* Mr. Wells! And I have a letter from you, asking me to call.'

Altogether, as you will have gathered, a forceful personality, and my heart went out to Wells as he gazed limply at Fraser, whose gleaming eyes proclaimed that he had sighted harbour just in time. His last shilling had gone on a night at Rowton House—'fine value they give you'—and the next move, he implied, was with Wells.

'Well, what can we do for him?' said Wells, in a high voice, turning to me. It occurred to me that a planned Fraser should be child's play to the creator of so many planned worlds, but as Wells continued to look at me appealingly, I said that perhaps a friend of mine, a manager in Heinz's Beans, might find a job for Fraser. Wells, on his side, said he would give Fraser a letter to Beaverbrook.

Wells having written his letter, and I having written mine, I felt that the kindest thing I could do would be to remove Fraser, together with myself.

A day or two later I heard from Fraser. My letter to the manager at Heinz's, which he enclosed, was, he said, no longer necessary. Thanks to Wells, he had made a wonderful start with the *Daily Express*. He was writing for it every day, and the enclosed cuttings, which he would be glad to have back, would show me what they were doing for him.

They had featured him as a youthful protégé of Wells's, who had come to London to make his fortune. The *Daily Express* was giving him his chance, and the readers of the *Daily Express* would read with interest the impression made by London on this fresh and alert young mind.

Two or three more days went by, and then I heard from Fraser again. Would I send him back the letter to the manager at Heinz's? The *Daily Express* had told him they could not do anything more for him. If he wanted to become a journalist, he must start in the provinces, like every one else.

He got a job at Heinz's, two pounds ten a week, chucked it in a month or two, and went to Germany. About three years later I heard from him again. He had, he told me, come back from Germany in an exalted mood, believing that a great political destiny lay before him. Reflection had suggested that he must prepare for this destiny with three years at Oxford. . . . I was unable to indicate any way of realizing this project, and though we exchanged a few letters on more general topics I gathered from his tone that he felt I had failed him. I have not heard from him since.

Fraser was, I suppose, an extreme example of the type attracted by Wells the Utopian. The extraordinary thing about Wells is that in spite of being ravaged by his Utopianism he managed to be the best novelist of his period.

Galsworthy and Walpole

Pearson: With Galsworthy as his only rival, and that only in popular esteem. Curiously enough, Galsworthy was also Shaw's only serious rival on the stage, but I doubt if posterity will value him there either. I was in two of his plays. While I was rehearsing the Major in his last play, *The Roof*, he came up to me and said: 'You remind me very much of an actor who once played Marlow in *The Silver Box.*' 'That's odd,' I replied, 'because you remind me very much of the author of *The Silver Box.*' 'But I *am* the author of *The Silver Box.*' 'And I am the actor who once played Marlow in it.'

Kingsmill: Not much happier than my only meeting with his successor, Hugh Walpole, whom I interviewed for *Hearth and Home.* At twenty-two one expects people to be pleased by the acuteness with which one analyses them. There was something oppressive about his luxurious flat in Hallam Street, and the oppression did not lift when he told me he always felt as if London were alive, as if it were a great monster which one day might shake the streets and houses from its back. In my interview I said that though mentally and to look at he was the ordinary public school product, his imagination was morbid, and I hinted that it would not surprise me if he ended in an asylum. What did surprise, and even hurt me, was that he complained about this interview to my brother Arnold.

I have sometimes thought that The Book Society might have been better disposed towards me if I had not put straws into its future President's hair.

The Chess Valley

Towards the close of his summer holidays Kingsmill returned from Somerset, to which his wife and family had moved, and reached London in time for the big air attack. After some days of it, he was glad to spend his last week-end before going back to Marlborough with Colin Hurry at Chipperfield. Pearson was living nearby in a cottage, and one afternoon walked with Kingsmill from Chorley Wood through the Chess Valley, where they had tea in a cottage garden. 'How wonderful this is!' Kingsmill exclaimed. 'I don't know whether it's the effect of listening to sirens making a noise like an ichthyosaurus in child-birth, plus the bizarre sensation of walking down Finchley Road at night with the same sounds and flashes about one as on the Somme, but this seems as lovely as the Lakes to me, and as far from London.' 'Lovelier than the Lakes,' replied Pearson, adding that one could never be sufficiently grateful to the motor-car for filling the Lakes and Devonshire with people who would otherwise be sprawling over the much more beautiful scenery at their back doors. 'Ken Wood,' he continued, 'is another instance. You may remember that a few years ago there was a threat of building on it. Owing to the opposition of several influential persons, it was saved for the nation, and predominantly for the inhabitants of London, whose millions flood Hampstead Heath next door to it, and are good enough to leave the glades of Ken Wood to me and half a dozen others.'

En Secondes Noces

Kingsmill, whom Pearson had previously told about the difficulties he was having over the Shaw biography, asked whether Shaw was still sitting on it. Shaw, said Pearson, was most anxious to get all the facts exactly right, and was looking at it daily. 'His secretary, Blanche Patch, tells me that he carries it about with him everywhere, and that she is constantly coming upon fragments of it scattered about the house. I get dollops of it back from him at irregular intervals, but he's only half-way through. He is also providing me with a lot of fresh data.'

Kingsmill: If you want any more, you can fit in a little story, revealing his human side, which I heard from Lillah MacCarthy. Do you know her?

Pearson: Yes. I have acted with her on several occasions.

Kingsmill: We met in Switzerland, and I sat with her one evening after dinner. I attempted to develop my idea of Shakespeare, but had less success than with Gollancz. Shakespeare, she said, with his brilliant mind and wonderful personality must— was it not clear from the Sonnets?—have been the centre of an adoring group of young aristocrats. We passed, not unwillingly on either side, to the parts she had played for G. B. S.—Ann in *Man and Superman*, and Lavinia in *Androcles*. Shaw, she said, had made a great mistake in not casting her for Joan. It was a part which demanded some one simple, passionate, primitive. What,

I asked, was Shaw like as a man? He had, she replied, a brilliant mind and wonderful personality. It was a delight to be with him, to hear him talk. Had he, I asked, any more specifically human qualities? Not for the world at large, she said, but for those who really knew him he was a different person. Once, at a difficult time in her life, she went to him for advice. He took her for a walk; it was night; and to raise her spirits he told her she must not let her mind dwell on the changes and chances of ordinary life— were there not always the stars?

Interesting, also, was a talk I had with another well-known actress, Lena Ashwell. I attempted to develop my idea of Shakespeare, and had taken Cleopatra as a starting-point, when she explained that the usual conception of Cleopatra as an immoral woman was entirely absurd, and in no way supported by the facts. Cleopatra married Julius Caesar. Julius Caesar died; and after a considerable interval she married Mark Antony. And there was nothing more to say.

Pearson: Mrs. Patrick Campbell would have welcomed that view, for, like Cleopatra, she also was married twice. Gabriel Pascal, who struck me when I met him as extremely tough, asked Shaw for an introduction to her when she was over seventy. Shaw gave him a letter, he called on her in Paris, was duly vamped, and when he came back raved about her, saying that he must put her into a Shavian film. But Shaw, who had once been in the toils of this Cleopatra, advised him to have nothing whatever to do with her.

Oddities and Characters

Kingsmill: She must have been a real character.

Pearson: Nonsense. She was only an oddity.

Kingsmill: In England oddities are called real characters. I quite agree with your implied distinction between the two.

Pearson: An oddity is a character without a centre. He has the qualities of a character, but they're floating about all over the place. The greatest of all oddities is Boswell, the greatest of all characters is Johnson.

Kingsmill: And with a character one feels that he needs all the balance and strength his centre gives him to prevent him collapsing into an oddity. If Johnson was a model to Boswell, Boswell was equally a warning to Johnson.

Pearson: Of course having character is not the same as being one. Washington had character, so had Lee, so, I suppose, had Pym and William of Orange, not to mention Sully, Seneca, Southey, Shaftesbury and Spinoza. But, God knows, none of them was a character.

Kingsmill: There are very few really great characters. Johnson, of course, and Beethoven, and Cromwell, and Carlyle.

Pearson: And Swift and Cervantes and Shaw and Sydney Smith.

Kingsmill: Frank Harris, after Boswell, is the greatest oddity I know of; and as a bundle of contradictory qualities he beats even Boswell.

Pearson: Coleridge is the genius as oddity.
Kingsmill: And Swinburne is the oddity as genius.

G. K. Chesterton

Pearson: My favourite contemporary oddity is G. K.
Chesterton. He was a dear old boy, and was very
helpful to me on two occasions, so I feel a little
remorse that I did not respond more genially to
what, none the less, I must regard as a symptom of

outstanding oddity on his part—his illusion that
when I called on him he saw before him a likely
convert to the Catholic faith. He had asked me
out to Beaconsfield, a Roman Catholic priest was
present at lunch, and afterwards the three of us sat
together in the garden. It was a lovely day, and the
roses were at their best. Gradually, but with no
assistance from me, the conversation drifted round
to religion, and G. K. C. remarked that all the
more intelligent writers in what he supposed he
must call the modern movement were becoming
Catholics. He instanced a few, and then, turning

to me, asked: 'And why are you not a Catholic? You are among the intelligent ones.'

'Perhaps I'm not quite intelligent enough,' I replied, wishing to evade the subject.

G. K. C. laughed, and said: 'We mustn't let you escape as easily as that.' The priest then took a hand: 'Is there anything in the teaching of the Church that stands in your way?'

'Everything,' I said.

'You do not believe in God, then?'

'Indeed I do. But I think the subject too big for popes, archbishops, convocations or cardinals. You cannot reduce God to a formula or a doctrine. And I think theologians are the last people to understand God, just as scholars are the last people to understand Shakespeare.'

'What is your conception of God?' demanded G. K. C.

His persistence rather ruffled me, and I replied: 'If I could give you my conception of God, I might have conceived him, and I assure you I didn't. But my private opinion is that he is a combination of oxygen, hydrogen and carbonic acid gas, with other substances thrown in to make him solid.'

'Well, well,' said the priest, 'we are getting nowhere. But you will come round to us in time.'

'If only you realized that in admiring those lovely roses you were nearer to God than when saying your masses, I should be with you in no time,' said I.

After the priest left I spent a very pleasant evening with G. K. C.

Kingsmill: The only time I met G. K. C. was when I interviewed him for *Hearth and Home*. He was amiable but vague. What chiefly struck me was the absence of beer and the presence of liqueurs, a form of alcohol which in his writings he consigned to the decadents and Oscar Wilde. In later years I saw him once or twice in Marylebone Station, drinking a glass of milk in his wife's company. My last sight of him was in the neighbourhood of Leicester Square on a hot summer day in 1929. He had come to rest opposite a somewhat pornographic bookshop, and was staring at the window with a look of unutterable dejection, not caused, I think, by the contents of the window, deplorable though he would have found them, but by a general weariness of everything.

Max Beerbohm

Kingsmill left Marlborough at the end of the Christmas term, and after some weeks with his family in Somerset spent a few days with Pearson at Chipperfield, arriving on January 9, 1941. It was his intention, as he was now about to become a non-resident master at Merchant Taylors, to use Chipperfield as a base from which to explore the environs of north-west London for rooms, but it was only on the day before he left Chipperfield that he put this design into execution.

'Any luck?' Pearson inquired when Kingsmill returned.

'If you can call it luck,' said Kingsmill gloomily. 'The circumference of London appears to be packed with people who don't want to be blown to bits in the centre. Natural enough from their standpoint, but it has put prices up, and I am paying more than I ought to for something far different from what I would like—a commercial hotel at Harrow, a gloomy place tenanted, so far as I could gather from a cursory glance, by homeless people who have given up all hope of a home from home, and ask for nothing better than a grave from the grave. There are times when I almost prefer the Edwardian age to this one. I see you are reading Max

Beerbohm's *Seven Men*. I have never wished him any particular harm, but after the day I have just had I find the thought of him a little provoking.'

Pearson: Too Edwardian for your present mood? He was certainly a finished product of that age. I met him once. It was not a very exciting meeting, and I am sure he has long forgotten it, though at the age of twenty-three I naturally found it thrilling enough. One day, after rehearsal at His Majesty's, Beerbohm Tree asked me to run up to his dressing-room and tell Max to join him for lunch at the Carlton, next door. When I entered the room Max was standing before a long mirror and regarding himself in an aloof, have-we-been-introduced sort of way. He seemed to be on the point of apologizing to himself for having been, in ever so slight a degree, a little too familiar with himself.

No one was with him, and though he noticed my arrival in the glass he did not turn round. I felt nervous, and cleared my throat loudly before speaking. He ignored the sound.

'Are you Mr. Beerbohm?' I asked, knowing perfectly well that he was, but not knowing how else to open the conversation. He did not reply. This annoyed me, and I repeated my question in perhaps too martial a tone.

'Have you a warrant for my arrest?' came the unexpected reply. He did not turn round, which annoyed me still more, and I said 'No' with curt severity. He gave an affected start, and asked: 'Have you brought the handcuffs?' This time I lost my temper, and fairly shouted 'No!' Turning, he said: 'Then I will come quietly.'

Being accustomed to this kind of thing at His Majesty's Theatre, his half-brother Tree having hardened me to it, I gave my message without any trimmings.

'Sounds like an ultimatum,' he murmured as he went towards the door, adding, just before he disappeared, something that sounded like 'Thank you, constable'. I suppose my nervousness had made my manner a little too stentorian. When I told Tree a little later in the day what had occurred his comment was 'Ah! you should have laughed'.

The Privacy of Englishmen

Kingsmill: Haven't you written an account of that meeting somewhere?

Pearson: I may have done, but thank you for reminding me that I have reached the chestnut age. I shall watch out for your lapses in future. To return to Max. I love his *Seven Men*: it's a perfect piece of work, easily the best thing he has ever done. People say he caricatures a quality of stand-offishness in Englishmen when he makes the two fellows in his *Laider* story maintain a week-long silence. But precisely the same thing once happened to me. In January 1930 I went with a theatrical company to America. The *Scythia* took about ten days to reach New York, touching at Belfast and at Halifax, Nova Scotia, on the way. For the greater part of those ten days I and another fellow, not a member of my company, spent our time in the smoking-room, and we were usually the sole occupants; but we never addressed a syllable or a nod to one another. Steaming up the Hudson, and passing the Statue of Liberty, I was standing on deck, having packed my luggage. Suddenly a voice at my side said 'Foggy morning'. I turned my head, and saw my silent companion of the smoking-room. The ice being broken, he rapidly told me the story of his life, just like Max's man. Such behaviour is therefore quite possible among Englishmen. It illustrates our intense individualism, our insistence on our own right to privacy, and the respect we pay to the rights of others. You also are a strong individualist; yet I cannot conceive your maintaining so much as a two-minute silence in a room with another man.

Kingsmill: There are different kinds of Englishmen. My father was extremely English, but being a Wesleyan he was steeped in the evangelizing sociability of that church. I do not mean that he would try to proselytize individuals. His evangelizing activities were all of an organizing kind, and based on collective action. But enough of the more primitive kind of evangelist remained in him to make him get into talk with any chance person he met in the course of his many travels. If you are right in saying that I am incapable of maintaining a two-minute silence in a room with another man, it must be from my father that I have inherited this trait. He could not even maintain the official two-minute silence, for one November the eleventh, when Arnold, a friend of his and myself were standing in a front room of the London office of our firm during the silence, my father rushed in, and seeing us grave, unspeaking, and immobile, exclaimed: 'What's happening? What is it?'

'It *was* the Two Minutes Silence,' Arnold replied.

'I think, however, that I am less sociable than I used to be. My curiosity about other people is dwindling. I am conscious of a less ardent desire to hear the stories of their lives from chance-met strangers. I still believe that every one is capable of being interesting about himself for half an hour, but nowadays, when I am on a train journey of an hour or upwards, I am no longer willing to be bored during the last part of the journey in consideration of having been entertained during the first part. So, as a rule, I shelter myself behind a book.

But I look back with pleasure on the more receptive period of my life. Even Englishmen, perhaps especially Englishmen, since they are so shut up at other times, tend to come out into the open during a train journey. The person addressed takes on the character of a representative of humanity as a whole. He is not any one in particular, he is merely a fellow-creature who has done and suffered enough to be able to follow with admiration or sympathy, according to the nature of the narrative, whatever experiences are poured into his ear.

The most unexpected confidence I ever received was on a journey from Dover to London. I was in the early thirties, and was returning from Switzerland, on a first-class pass. My fellow-passenger was a man of about fifty. From his suit-case, his clothes and his quiet assured manner he was obviously a man of means and position. We fell into conversation, the talk for most of the journey being of a general kind. But when we were within half an hour or so of London his remarks became rather disconnected, and I was about to open a book when he suddenly said: 'I am going back to my wife.' I inclined my head slightly, to indicate that if he wished to enlarge this statement he had my attention.

'My life with her is a hell,' he continued, in a

stern indignant voice. 'She is insanely jealous, and without any reason whatsoever—any valid reason. She is a very handsome woman, dark, with a Spanish strain, which no doubt accounts for her temperament. I am not allowed to have any interest, any thought even, of my own. Before I left on this journey, on the very evening before, she chased me round the dining-room table with the carving knife.

'That is what I am returning to. It is an impossible situation.'

My incoherent murmurings having died away, we sat in silence for the rest of the journey. As we entered Victoria Station, he shook himself, and going into the corridor directed a porter to take his suit-case and call a taxi. We got out of the train, and for a moment were standing side by side. Turning a cold eye on me, he said 'Good afternoon,' and walked away with the air of a man who knew how to defend his privacy.

Winston Churchill

Later in the evening, repairing to the bar of the Two Brewers Hotel, on Chipperfield Common, Pearson and Kingsmill heard some eulogistic references over the wireless to Winston Churchill.

Pearson: The people who thought hanging too good for Winston a couple of years ago now speak of

him as if he combined all the finer qualities of
the Deity. H. T. Muggeridge, who was M.P.
for Romford, told me that round about 1930
Winston was so unpopular with the Tories in the
House of Commons that they would not even
make room for him on the front bench.
Muggeridge saw him one day squeezing himself
down between two members, the space between
whom hardly afforded room for half a man; and
neither of them budged an inch until it was a
question of yielding or being crushed. No one
and nothing short of Hitler could have brought
him to power, though when I and about a thousand
others shook hands with him at a political meeting
in the days of Edward the Peacemaker, he was
considered a very promising politician.

Kingsmill: If ever in the history of the world one man
has earned another's ecstatic and imperishable
gratitude, Hitler has earned Winston's. There
should be flower-wreathed portraits of Hitler in
every room that Winston enters. A tress from
Hitler's head should lie in a locket against his
heart. Two years ago his life was a confused
mosaic, with some brilliant splashes of colour here
and there. Had he died then, who would have
remembered him in even fifty years? About
as many people as remember his father now. His
chief claim to remembrance was Gallipoli, but
posterity does not devote much thought to cam-
paigns which would have been brilliant triumphs
if they had not been complete failures.

Now he is certain of one of the highest places
in our history. As a boy he may have dreamed of

rallying England in some terrible hour, when every other nation had gone down before an irresistible Attila, but what would he have thought if you had told him ten years ago that his erratic and inconclusive career, then already petering out, would suddenly, in his later sixties, take an upward leap, and place him beside Chatham and Nelson, well above Marlborough, and far above Lloyd George? I am not even sure that, as men of action are remembered more for their setting than for themselves, he won't eventually stand out more vividly than any other leader in our history. Chatham had no Hitler to see to the limelight, and England was not in such a tight corner before Trafalgar as after Dunkirk.

Pearson: Never before has one man owed so much to another. But do you think he is conscious of what he owes to Hitler?

Kingsmill: If he could be, he wouldn't owe it.

Pearson: Cryptic.

Kingsmill: I am sure he loathes Hitler as much as he says. He sees everything in black and white, and that's why last June gave him the chance he took so magnificently. You say you are on the watch for my chestnuts, but as Winston has been much in my thoughts of late, may I give you a fuller account of my meeting with him than you have yet had?

Pearson: That's fair, after Max.

Kingsmill: It was at a Naval Division dinner, in 1924, I think. As Frank Harris's future biographer, I felt I ought not to miss this chance of getting Winston's view of him. Harris, according to

Harris, had once known Winston fairly intimately, but of course that was nothing much to go by, and even if there were any truth in the claim I was conscious that a Naval Division dinner, with its high regrets and heroic memories, was not the occasion on which to switch Winston over to a blackmailer and a pro-German. But I decided that if a chance presented itself, I must take it.

Dinner over, a group of about a dozen collected round Winston, listening intently to his serious remarks, and greeting what were no doubt his amusing ones with respectful laughter. After half an hour or so of this, Winston signified his intention to leave them for a few moments, a lane was formed, and he swept down it, and out of the room. Following him, I stationed myself at the entrance to the lavatory, and waited anxiously for zero hour. As he approached me on his way back, I cleared my throat, and as he drew level I said: 'Excuse me. I believe you knew Frank Harris.' Swinging round, some surprise and more irritation in his light blue eyes, he snapped 'Yes'.

'I am thinking of writing his life, and I should be very glad if you would give me your opinion of him.'

'He was a brilliant writer. He wrote the best article that appeared in the Press when my father died.'

'What do you think of him as a man of action? Do you think he had possibilities in that direction?'

Winston made an impatient gesture. 'He was a pro-German. He went over to America, and wrote against us.'

'Yes, but . . .'

'He was a traitor. He betrayed his own country. I can't forgive him that.' The impatience which had been mounting rapidly within him during this brief interchange exploded, and he surged away, calling out over his shoulder: 'I wouldn't write his life!'

I only hope that, when the war is over, he leaves office as quickly as he left me. He has done one thing as well as any man in our history could have done it, and it would be a pity if he spoiled the effect.

Baldwin and Beaverbrook

Pearson: No one in our political history has made his exit at the right moment, except Baldwin.

Kingsmill: What a shower of dead cats he had the wit to miss!

Pearson: And four years ago, he was every one's hero—it seems incredible now.

Kingsmill: I wonder what he thinks of Winston's apotheosis, not to mention the lesser but quite substantial glory of Beaverbrook.

Pearson: Who, apparently, disliked Baldwin from the word go. I heard an amusing story the other day of Baldwin's effect on Beaverbrook when they first met. In the days when Bonar Law was Prime Minister, Baldwin and Beaverbrook used to go along in the evenings for a smoke and a chat with him. Whenever Bonar Law knocked out the ashes of his pipe against the firegrate, Baldwin used to say: 'Come in'. After several months this got on Beaverbrook's nerves. And when Baldwin rose to go, he used always to say: 'Well, time for Bedfordshire.' After several months this, too, got on Beaverbrook's nerves.

Kingsmill: He shouldn't have let himself be rattled. If he'd retorted 'Rutland for me', he might have done Baldwin out of the succession to the premiership.

Pearson: Did I ever tell you that my father was partly responsible for Baldwin?

Kingsmill: I am glad to hear it. That is a responsibility which should be divided between as many people as possible. But how?

Pearson: My father was on the Worcester Conservative Committee which invited Baldwin's father to stand for parliament. That settled the son's future. My father told me that Baldwin was then a shy reserved young man with gingerish hair, and gave no indication of the future king-breaker.

The Light Ages

Towards the close of January Kingsmill, anxious for a respite from his hotel, spent a week-end at Chipperfield.

'We eat at small tables in my morgue,' he lamented to his friend, 'and I am at a table with a married couple in the late fifties. They sit facing one another, and I am in between. The weather and the latest air raid occupy the first two minutes of the meal, and then there is complete silence. I thought I could bear it better if I were not between them, so last night I said to the wife: "Wouldn't you prefer to sit next your husband?" "No, thank you," she replied. There was no feeling in her voice. If she had been expressing the accumulated hatred of thirty years, I could at least have felt that I was suffering in the interests of a fellow-creature. But she appears rather to like her husband than not. Her tone when she says "Have you had a good day?" is almost affable. What can you do with a race like this? If Ribbentrop had put up at my place, he would have advised Hitler to better purpose. But let's talk about something civilized. How are Shaw and Shakespeare?'

Pearson: I've finished my biography of Shakespeare, and Shaw has at last finished with my biography of him. I shall now revise it thoroughly, and I hope it will come out in the autumn, though it might be wiser to hold it up till after the war.

Kingsmill: Why wait till then? War or peace, the English are, always have been, and always will be, pure teak.

Pearson: Except in the Dark Ages, and I devoutly hope that we shall have another spell of them when the war's over.

Kingsmill: ?

Pearson: The so-called Dark Ages occurred after the departure of the Romans from Britain, and before the coming of the Christians. In this happy interlude our ancestors were bullied neither by the departed organization, the State, nor by the impending one, the Church. There is no record

116

of that time, because contented people do not require institutions to make them feel secure, nor historians to make them feel important. If record were found, it was destroyed by the clergy and politicians, who knew that they would lose their jobs if it got about that people were happy without them. So in the interests of both, the Dark Ages had to be kept dark. We should really call them the Light Ages, when human beings spent their

carefree, irresponsible and wholly joyful lives rocking to and fro on their velvet arses in a condition of ungovernable mirth and inextinguishable high spirits. Have another drink?

Warmed by a second whisky, Kingsmill said that he had perhaps exaggerated the painfulness of his surroundings. 'There is a pleasant fellow of thirty-five or so, with whom I occasionally exchange a few remarks. I think the reason Englishmen are so dumb is because they have more poetry in them than other people, and being frightened of it keep it in some inaccessible subterranean region, out of which it occasionally throws a jet into the upper air. After some evenings of desultory chat with this fellow, he told me that he felt he had missed life. Nothing had ever happened to him, and he was certain nothing ever would. After all, he was thirty-five—it was too late to begin living now. I told him I had found life much more interesting since thirty-five than before, but he shook his head. Last Sunday he turned up to breakfast after ten, and when I asked him why he was so late, he answered, rather poetically, as it seems to me: "I have been lying in bed, thinking of all that has been, and of all that will never be."'

Harrow-on-the-Hill

Towards the end of April, having completed his labours on the life of Shaw, Pearson left Chipperfield with his wife and settled down at Whatlington, near Battle, in Sussex, where a house, Woods Place, had been put at their disposal. Kingsmill meanwhile had left his Harrow boarding-house for Northwood, and after spending his Easter holidays with his family in Somerset, had returned to Northwood for the summer term.

One Saturday in June he went down to Whatlington for a night at The Mill House, where his friend Malcolm Muggeridge lived. Muggeridge, who was on a short leave from Salisbury, having taken his children to the coast for a dip, Pearson and Kingsmill walked into Battle for tea, which they had in the garden of the Gateway teashop, overlooking a valley on one of whose slopes some cows were browsing. 'No place in the world like

England,' said Kingsmill. 'I wish we could do our Shakespeare book. Two and a half years already since the Cotswolds, and our tribute to Shakespeare still undelivered. Can anything be done about it?' After some discussion Pearson said he would come up on the following Thursday, spend the night at Northwood, and go into the matter at length.

From Northwood, where the friends met on the 26th of June, Kingsmill took Pearson to Harrow, in execution of a long-threatened intention to show him the scenes of his schooldays. It was Pearson's first visit to Harrow-on-the-Hill since his youth, when he had sometimes walked there on Sundays from Hampstead through leafy lanes, Golder's Green still in the country, Hendon a secluded village, and the view from the church at Harrow unblurred by any of the red buildings that now stretched for miles in every direction.

Going through a narrow passage-way Kingsmill remarked: 'I don't expect you to dance with excitement over what I am about to tell you, but this is the way my father used to go to and from the railway station every morning for twenty years or so. Last January, when I used to come along here in the dark mornings, the thought of all the enterprises which once buzzed in his head as he hastened this way saddened me. When a man of affairs and action dies, little or nothing seems left as a memorial of his resource and ingenuity and energy. If his business outlasts him, he is only an empty name; if it doesn't, he isn't even that. It was like Hamlet to maunder over Yorick's skull, but the mere idea of Yorick warms one, though none of his jokes survive. "Alas, poor Fortinbras!" would have been more to the point.'

As they crossed the slope below the church, Kingsmill was moved to a further reminiscence. 'Sir Frederic Kenyon, who was the keeper of the manuscripts in the British Museum, used to come this way. Keeping manuscripts probably does not go with a strong desire for small talk just after breakfast. At any rate, my father used frequently to complain that Kenyon walked too fast for him. He did not put the suspicion into words, but there was something in the tone of his complaint which suggested a doubt whether Kenyon was naturally a fast walker.'

Passing through an alley, they came out into a street, a yard or two behind a tall thin man whose lined face, drooping shoulders and blank stare gave an impression of extreme age. 'I say,' Kingsmill whispered to Pearson, 'I know that chap. He used to be a friend of mine. He's one of our contemporaries.' Pearson, who had been stepping out vigorously, gave a startled grunt, but recovering himself squared his shoulders again.

In front of the pavilion on the sixth form cricket ground, two or three members of the cricket eleven were fooling about in a way which recalled memories to Kingsmill. 'They seem very much the same type as the bloods of thirty-five years ago,' he said. 'I find it difficult to believe that Harrow is the only public school which hasn't improved since the beginning of the century, but the good athletes at Marlborough and Merchant Taylors haven't any of the bumptiousness of those fellows. I think there really must be a Harrow type, and the fact that the school is now only half as big as before the Great War suggests that the world of to-day has less room for that type than it once had. Harrow, as I remember it, was a first-rate example of the extreme divergence between practice and sentiment in the Victorian age. Hence its famous school songs, which, as compared with the reality, were Little Nell to Mrs. Charles Dickens.'

They examined Kingsmill's old home from the outside, climbed the hill, and after a glance at a house in which Kingsmill had lived for a few months, but which he excused his friend from surveying with particular attention, they went up a drive to the site of Anthony Trollope's old home, Orley Farm, now taken down, but in Kingsmill's early years the quarters of his preparatory school. A wonderful view over North London solaced Pearson for the Odyssey to which his friend had exposed him, and they strolled peacefully back to the King's Head, where, after an admirable dinner, they sat on the terrace, drinking coffee and smoking. It was a lovely evening, and they could see the distant Berkshire hills.

Pearson: I can't have been more than twenty-one when I last saw that view. Life stretched before me, and seemed as wonderful as the scene then was, fresh, unspoilt, varied and enticing. All the houses that have since sprung up in that landscape remind me of the obstacles and disillusionments of my pilgrimage.

Kingsmill: Disillusionment is the result of discovering that other people are as egotistical as oneself.

Pearson: True, if inharmonious at the moment.

Kingsmill: Sorry. To put my point more gradually, we all tend to think of the world as a vast entity rolling along in brutish indifference to our demands on it. But after all the world is only a number of individuals, each desiring preferential treatment, and expecting to find in others the perfection he himself does not possess. That is why youth is so painful, because when we 'go out into the world', as the phrase is, we think that it will be something entirely different from what we have already experienced. The tragedy of adolescence is not that it discovers, but that it rediscovers, what life is like.

To me that landscape recalls the many evenings I spent looking out over it towards Ireland, where Cecily, who at that time embodied perfection for me, lived at Hillside. Every Hillside is both a dream and a reality. I have given you an account of the reality of one Hillside. But, like Le Beau, who may or may not have been speaking for Shakespeare, I believe in 'a better world than this' and that there the present reality of our Hillsides will be a forgotten dream, and the dream will have become the reality.

Pearson: Whether Le Beau was or was not speaking for Shakespeare, oughtn't we to be speaking about him? Our retrospective ramblings are diverting us from the business of the day—namely, what is our book to be about? As I said at Battle, having just got Shakespeare off my chest, I do not favour making him our main theme. Nor do such publishers as we have consulted on the matter. While you were talking just now, I was much struck by the otherwise unbroken tranquillity of this scene. Here we are, within ten minutes of the German aerodromes in France—a terrace dotted with semi-somnolent fellow-countrymen, enjoying a summer evening such as only England knows. I suggest England as our theme.

Kingsmill: Excellent. And much more likely than Shakespeare to appeal to a publisher, especially as England is at the moment so much in the air. Well put, that.

Pearson: And of course we can drag in Shakespeare as often as we like.

Kingsmill: We can start with our Cotswold journey, and then proceed with no settled plan. It would be unEnglish to deal with our subject systematically. As we are both English, it is reasonable to assume that England will emerge from the book. I do not say the whole of England, but much more than if we were both French. It will be a book from which a sensitive reader will be able to infer England. That gets it. *Infer* England.

Having settled their theme, and Pearson having said he would look in at Methuen's the next day and see Alan White about it, they rose, and walked along the High Street through the still lingering day.

Hilaire Belloc

'That large red building,' said Kingsmill, 'is the school Speech Room—prize-givings, end-of-term concerts, and so on. I never see it without remembering a really wonderful lecture Belloc gave in it, I think in 1905. He was half an hour late, and a lesser man might have had a rough reception. But he strode to the centre of the platform, and in a slightly French accent, which added a note of ferocity to his words, barked out: "I am half an hour late. It is entirely my fault. I do not apologize." He then lectured on London, evoking it in earlier centuries with a rich imaginative power that gave me an impression of genius such as I have received from no other speaker. What an extraordinary man he is! If there is anything in reincarnation, there was a muddle in the laboratory when Belloc was re-issued in his present form. He ought to have come back as Rabelais, with a dash of du Bellay. But one of the laboratory assistants, deaf or daft, mistook his instructions, and blended Rabelais with Torquemada.'

Pearson: I once heard Belloc stop a politician talking, and a man who can do that is equal to anything. Somewhere in the nineteen-twenties I was one of a crowd of cricketers at Rodmell in Sussex. Belloc had come over to watch the match, and afterwards we forgathered at Murray Allison's house nearby. While we were all enjoying Belloc's wit and unpublished verse, the Liberal candidate for a neighbouring constituency walked in, and began to drivel about politics. He talked and talked, and nothing could stop him. He told us of his life's struggles, of his attempts to liberalize the community, of his friendships with the eminent. Belloc sat motionless and silent throughout. As an ex-M.P., he had received a good training, for the man who has survived a year of the House of Commons is beyond boredom. The rest of us coughed, lit matches noisily, tried weakly to interrupt, but were easily talked down. The Liberal candidate would probably have come to a

sticky end if Belloc had not saved him. At a moment when he had to draw breath or burst, Belloc, looking innocently at the ceiling, suddenly asked in that high quick voice of his:

'Have you ever heard the story of the male and female contortionists on their honeymoon?'

There was a pause, during which the politician, his mouth open, stared at Belloc. 'I—I beg your pardon?' he spluttered.

'Have you ever heard the story of the male and female contortionists on their honeymoon?'

'N-no.'

'They broke it off.'

So did the politician.

'This Blessed Plot'

A fortnight later Alan White and Kingsmill lunched with Pearson at his club.

'It is difficult to give a cut-and-dried idea of the book,' said Kingsmill, after he had been talking for some minutes without conveying anything in particular beyond his enjoyment of his Cotswold journey, his love of Shakespeare, and his appreciation of his native land. 'Our aim is to write a book from which the reader will be able to *infer* England.'

White: Infer?

Kingsmill: Gather.

Pearson: The book is bound to contain a lot about us. That can't be helped. Every man's his own England.

Kingsmill: Always provided that he is an Englishman.

White: What are you going to call it?

Pearson: Why not *Between You and Me*?

White: Or, more simply, 'The Gatepost'.

Kingsmill: I think that the title, at least, should have something to do with England. There must be something suitable in the poets.

Pearson: There's only one poet, and most of his patriotic phrases have already been pinched. Shall we comb John of Gaunt's speech in *Richard II*, and see if our fellow-scribes have left anything for us. Ah! I have it: 'This teeming womb of royal kings.' That's fine! 'This teeming womb' would make a pregnant title.

White: First-rate, as a counterblast to Marie Stopes.

Kingsmill: Try something else.

Pearson: I'll recite the whole speech if you like.

Kingsmill: I can stand a lot in the interests of our joint enterprise.

Pearson:
'This happy breed of men, this little world,
This precious stone set in the silver sea. . . .'

Kingsmill: 'This Precious Stone'—I like that.

White: Isn't it a little too——

Kingsmill: Precious? Perhaps you're right. Forge ahead, Hesketh.

Pearson:
'This Blessed Plot, this . . .'

Kingsmill: Stop! 'This Blessed Plot'—you can't beat that.

White: Yes, that's not at all bad.

Kingsmill: It expresses our feeling, it will ensnare readers of thrillers, and it will give you, Hesketh, an opportunity to recur to your recent exploits with fork and spade.

Pearson: Not that I have ever called any of the plots I've been digging 'blessed'.

White: Have you been digging for victory, too?

Pearson: No, for gluttony.

Kingsmill: Strange—it never occurred to me before that digging for victory had its compensations. Well, Alan, you have the title, and I can guarantee that none of our readers will guess the plot, even when they've reached the end of the book.

Bedlam

Everything thus clarified, the talk drifted to other topics, and Pearson asked Kingsmill if he had read of the recent death of a fellow-clubman whom they had both known.

Pearson: I shall always remember him because he introduced me to Bedlam.

Kingsmill: Bedlam!

White: Bedlam?

Pearson: Bedlam. I was leaving the club late one night when the porter, an admirable person whatever he may once have been as a sergeant-major, came up to me and asked whether I would drop a friend at his home in Bedford Park. My home being in St. John's Wood, I wanted to know why my friend could not drop himself.

'Well, sir, 'e's come over queer like,' said the porter.

This was another way of saying that he was speechlessly drunk. Rather against my will I agreed, and together we supported him into a taxi. Giving his address to the driver, I made a few fruitless attempts to converse with him, and then lay back in my seat wondering how, without appearing too much of a prig, I could make it clear to his wife that I was not responsible for his condition. The most difficult thing in the world is to break the news to a wife that her husband is horizontally tight, while managing at the same time to convey: 1. That you are entirely innocent in this case; 2. That you have frequently been drunk yourself; 3. That drink doesn't take you in that way; 4. That your sympathy is with the unfortunate fellow; 5. That your sympathy is with his wife; 6. That it's an awful pity; and 7. That nevertheless men are men.

While I was musing on the problem, the taxi had got as far as Hyde Park Corner, at which point my friend came to with a start, and began seeing all sorts of things which to my more sober eye were not apparent. Most of the things had no doubt been observed by him at one time or another in the reptilian portion of the Zoo, but there was no sign of them at Hyde Park Corner. He babbled on so incoherently, so frantically, and in fact so foamingly that the story I had been quietly piecing together for his wife had to be discarded. This was not an occasion for an explanation which could only hold water. So I told the driver to return to the club, where, asking him to keep an eye on his fare, I broke the news to the porter, whose experience in similar situations might, I fancied, come in useful.

'Take 'im straight off to Bedlam, sir,' said the porter.

I focused him very carefully, wondering whether he had been drinking, too.

'To where?'

'To Bedlam, sir. There's not a minute to lose.'

It occurred to me that lunacy was catching. I had caught it from my friend, whose ravings I could hear through the swing-doors, and the porter had caught it from me. I pulled myself together, took a deep breath, and spoke firmly:

'Now look here. Let's get this straight. You and I are sober. But Mr. —— is not. In fact he is delirious. I cannot take him home in that condition. What do you advise me to do?'

'I'm *tellin'* you, sir. Take 'im to Bedlam. The boss there is a pal of 'is.'

There must have been something strange in my expression, because he came out of his office and drew me towards the entrance.

'Now you come along o' me, sir. I'll settle it all right.'

He hustled me out, bawled at the taxi-driver 'Bedlam! Quick!' and after telling me to ask for 'The Master' when I got there, banged the door on me.

I cannot for the life of me remember where we went. My mind was in a whirl, and I kept saying 'Bedlam? Bedlam?' as if the repetition would in time make things clear. At last the taxi stopped, and I had another shock when the driver, opening the door at a blank grey wall, announced 'Bedlam, sir'.

In spite of the reality of my friend's presence, which was reinforced by the distressing sounds that issued from his mouth, I could not rid myself of the feeling that I was the victim of a more than usually macabre nightmare, and after ringing a squeaky bell I hit the door hard with my hand to see if I was awake. I seemed to be. The door was opened by a man who looked more like a head waiter than the demon or maniac I had expected to see. I asked for the Master, giving the name of my friend, who was instantly admitted —at least not quite instantly, for the strenuous assistance of the driver and myself was required to get him in.

I gathered that he had been there before, and further inquiries elicited the fact that Bedlam was short for Bethlehem, the name of the madhouse familiar to me in eighteenth century memoirs. Don't you think it most extraordinary that after knocking about the universe for twenty years I should have remained in complete ignorance that Bedlam really existed?

Kingsmill: I do indeed. But what came home to me most in your story was your analysis of the feelings of a drunken person's custodian. A job equally responsible and invidious. I remember, shortly after the last war, going up to Oxford to see a great friend, who had been in captivity with me, and was liable to terrific bouts of drinking. It was a week off the end of the term, and he told me he had hardly touched a drop during the previous two months. We had a bottle of wine at dinner, he saw me off the next day, and I thought no more of the matter. A week later I met him in my club, looking very desperate. The bottle we had shared, he told me, had set him going, and he had drunk almost without intermission ever since seeing me off. The hundred pounds his father had just sent him, to last some months, had all gone, he hadn't a penny, the two fellows he had been drinking with had been wheeled off on trucks at Paddington, and he himself had walked to the club. 'You certainly have a marvellous head,' I said. 'I can see you are fairly well away, because I know you so well, but I should never have suspected that you had put away a hundred pounds' worth since last week.' 'I wish to God I had your head, Hughie,' he groaned. 'If drink knocked me out, it wouldn't harm me.' 'Well, old man,' I replied, 'my head, such as it is, is at your disposal. What are your plans?'

He spent the night at my place, and the next afternoon I went to a hotel in Kensington, where his father was staying, a grim Scot who had been in the Indian Civil Service, and whom I had met once, and not greatly taken to. Like you, I framed reassuring explanations on my way down. His parents were in the lounge, and on seeing me started up, his mother, who had a sweet face, in great distress. 'John was to have been here last night,' she exclaimed. 'Has anything happened?' 'Nothing serious,' I said, 'but perhaps if I could have a word with your husband . . .'

The old boy drew me aside, and demanded sharply: 'Well, what is it?' Rather annoyed, I jettisoned my tact and replied: 'I suppose you know your son drinks.' 'I know nothing of the kind.' 'Well, I suppose you remember you sent him a hundred pounds a week ago.' 'Yes! Yes!' 'It's spent.'

I expected an explosion, but the effect was the exact opposite. As much sobered by the disappearance of the hundred pounds as his son had been the reverse, he led me to an alcove, and listened to what I had to say with the same attention as he had no doubt brought to tangled situations in the North-West Provinces. There was something impressive about the quickness with which he cut his losses, and concentrated on the measures necessary to minimize future risks.

Dogs and Cats

Term over, Kingsmill went down to Whatlington to work on the book with Pearson, arriving on July 28th. Pearson met him at Battle station; they took the bus to Whatlington, and walked up a long lane, leading from the Old Mill to Woods Place. Half-way up the lane a dog barked furiously at them from a farm on their left.

Pearson: I'm afraid you'll hear that dog every time you pass this house. It has contracted a habit of barking for barking's sake, its bark changing to a sycophantic whine if you go in and stroke it. Like Sydney Smith, I have no use for dogs. At one moment they bark and bully; at another they creep and crawl.

Kingsmill: *Dogs versus cats* is a theme on which fourth forms have a good deal to say. But I am interrupting you.

Pearson: The popularity of dogs is due to the fact that people love anything they can dominate, anything that is wholly dependent on them and adds to their prestige. A dog looks up to a man whom no human being will look up to. To a dog a man is a dog spelt backwards. Any fool can be a god to a dog, which is why every fool likes dogs.

I don't mind the brutes when they leave me alone; but I dislike having to be dog-conscious as an alternative to tripping over them whenever I move about the house; I hate their pestering habits; I detest the necessity of attending to them and of constantly exercising my will on them; and as I am incapable of hitting them they soon reduce me to a condition of distracted imbecility. No— give me a cat! There's a beautiful animal for you! It is clean, unlike a dog. Its habits are hygienic, unlike a dog's. It is independent, unlike a dog. It is quiet and restful, unlike a dog. It is self-contained, meditative, graceful, noiseless, friendly without being fawning, unobtrusive, self-sufficient, aloof and inscrutable—utterly unlike a dog—and moreover one does not have to take it out for walks or treat it as a born fool like a dog. All the finest types of creation prefer a cat to a dog. Dr. Johnson preferred a cat. Cats prefer cats.

Kingsmill: I have no particular feeling about either cats or dogs, but in pursuance of my duty as a schoolmaster I have noted with attention the points made by my pupils for and against each of those animals. Against dogs it has been urged that they are too big, and that they bark and growl; in their favour that they will carry things, that they can communicate their feelings more clearly than cats, that they are more friendly, that you can teach them to play, and that they show sympathy by licking your face. A point made against cats was that they were sly, and that they could not be taught to play unless brought up with dogs, which seemed to show that they were weaker— whether mentally, morally or physically I forgot to inquire. In their favour, they caught mice, they were soft and small, they didn't charge at one, they landed right if dropped, and they rubbed themselves against their mistress's legs.

Woods Place

Situated on what the eighteenth century writers call a gentle eminence, fields sloping down from it on three sides into valleys through which small trout-streams meander, and immediately beyond which rise low hills, rich with trees, pasture lands and wheat fields, and over everything a sense of freshness from the not far distant sea, Woods Place seemed to Kingsmill an ideal place in which to remember that the subject of their book was England. Its architecture, too, Pearson informed him, covered some centuries of island history, the rear part of the building consisting of a Tudor farmhouse, the front part having been added in the early part of the nineteenth century.

After he had taken Kingsmill to his bedroom in the Tudor wing, and warned him of the beams which must have bruised many heads in their time, Pearson showed him the room in which they were to work, directly over the front-door porch. 'If you can't write on England with that view in front of you,' said Pearson, 'you'll never be able to. On the other hand, with that view in front of you, you'll have a good excuse for not writing on anything.'

P. G. Wodehouse

Picking up a *Picture Post* after supper, Kingsmill came upon P. G. Wodehouse's broadcast from Berlin to the States. Having read it, he said: 'I'd like to see the trial of P. G. for high treason, urged by a correspondent in the *Daily Telegraph*, pivoting on this broadcast. P. G. is obviously living in his own Bertie-Wooster world. Much of this broadcast is quite as fantastic as anything in his stories, and might puzzle the counsel for the prosecution, though of course a leading K.C. has his own brand of fantasy, and I dare say could get as white-hot about this as about anything else.'

Pearson: If P. G. had spoken about the Germans in that vein at the time of his capture, I doubt if there'd have been much fuss. One must remember that he has been out of the war since it ceased to be phoney.

Kingsmill: Yes, our hatred of Germany sprang up as

soon as we thought there was a chance of their doing here what they have been doing elsewhere since the beginning of the war.

Pearson: What makes the Wodehouse affair so interesting is the way his brother humorists fell upon him.

Kingsmill: It appears from the letters of Milne and Darlington in the *Telegraph* that, in spite of their love for Wodehouse, they were always distressed and sometimes disgusted when they met him. Since this was so, why didn't they take their friend aside in some quiet evening hour, and before it was too late open before him the abyss of non-civic irresponsibility into which he was blindly sliding?

Pearson: Bentley on the other hand seems less concerned with Wodehouse the man than with
Wodehouse the Doctor of Letters. In spite of
Belloc having once announced that P. G. is the
greatest living master of English prose, Bentley
wants Oxford to cancel the degree they gave
him.

Kingsmill: And it was obvious from his letter that it
was less his patriotism that spoke than his wounded
faith in Oxford as a judge of literature. He com-
plains that one of the highest literary distinctions in
the world should be bestowed on a man who had
never written a serious line.

Pearson: A grave charge to bring against a humorist.

Kingsmill: It was typically donnish fun, honouring
P. G. No one but Bentley would be surprised at
it. And one can't blame Oxford for failing to
foresee that P. G. would become a hissing and a
by-word, as he himself would put it. Since Hitler
got properly loose, there isn't such a thing as a safe
wicket. If there were, Oxford would be playing
on it.

Pearson: I'd give a good deal to have been present at
the extraordinary meeting of The Drones Club last
month, after they had heard about the Master's
goings-on in Berlin. All the safest people in
England, including a Law Lord and the Public
Orator of Oxford . . .

Kingsmill: Found on their knees before a man whose
head on a charger was being demanded by an
outraged public.

Pearson: I was saddened to see that Sean O'Casey
joined the chorus of vituperation. After all, he has

written at least one play which is as good as anything since Shakespeare. I can't understand a man
of his intelligence trying to outbellow the rest of
that crowd.

Kingsmill: Well, he's an Irishman, and P. G. has become
an oppressed minority, and I suppose he couldn't
resist the temptation.

Pearson: Most of these people seem to think that
Wodehouse is under an obligation to the public,
but, as the critics always used to reiterate, the public
is under an unrepayable obligation to him—unrepayable till they got the chance of repaying it
with bad eggs and dead cats.

Kingsmill: Did you see Janus in *The Spectator*? I have
been carrying it about with me for some days, and
it runs as follows: 'I have never till to-day been
rather thankful that Lord Oxford—Mr. Asquith—
is dead. But I am glad he did not live to see a
writer he so unreservedly admired as he did Mr.
P. G. Wodehouse broadcasting from a German
station.' Asquith died in 1928. Since then there
has been the biggest slump in history, beginning
with twelve millions unemployed and starving in
the States.

Pearson: The inhabitants of China have been bombed
in hundreds of thousands and drowned in millions.

Kingsmill: The natives of Abyssinia have been exter-
minated by the Italians, which I need hardly say
implies a disparity in armament unparalleled in war.

Pearson: Spain has been decimated by fratricidal strife.

Kingsmill: The Russian peasantry has been immolated
to further the millennium.

Pearson: And there has also been Hitler.

Kingsmill: But Mr. Asquith, according to Janus, would have felt no desire to turn his face to the wall until he unexpectedly heard the once-loved voice of P. G. Wodehouse speaking from Berlin.

D. L. Murray

Pearson: Of course there were two or three people who wrote about P. G. in a sensible civilized way —Gilbert Frankau and Monckton Hoffe, and I remember a witty and pointed letter from a Manchester correspondent, Walter James.

Kingsmill: And then there was the *Times Lit. Sup.* which asked for a suspension of judgement. That must have been D. L. Murray.

Pearson: Very decent of him. But then he's not a well-known humorist; he's only got a sense of humour. He once made me roar with laughter over a Fleet Street lunch—but you've heard this already.

Kingsmill: Never mind. I can always hear it again.

Pearson: He told me he used to go night after night to see Martin Harvey in *The Corsican Brothers,* simply for one moment, at the end of the play, when the hero, who in his dual capacity has been cornering the limelight throughout, is now stamping up and down, threatening to tear the villain to bits and scatter the fragments to the four winds. The villain, who by this time has only got one foot on the stage, mutters 'Pitiful boaster!', whereupon the hero, slap in a full blaze of light, stares all about with incredulous amazement, and with a shattered howl demands: 'Gentlemen—*Do* I look like a boooaaaster?'

Then there was that other story, which you may also be glad to hear again. Murray was acting with Estelle Stead's Shakespearean company. Her leading man produced the plays, and tended to be very liverish at early rehearsals. One morning he

came down in a particularly disgruntled mood to rehearse the gravediggers scene in *Hamlet*. The two clowns went through their traditional stuff with dreary exactitude—you can picture it, 10 a.m., a bare stage, and two actors drooping in their ordinary clothes. At the conclusion of the dismal procedure, the producer, fixing them with loathing in his eyes, and baring his teeth, snarled venomously: 'You're *not* funny. You *don't* amuse me. Make me *laugh*, can't you? MAKE ME LAUGH!'

And these were only two of at least half a dozen stories, all really brilliantly told.

Kingsmill: Looking at an old diary the other day, I was surprised how often Murray's name occurred. That was at Oxford in 1910. But the tides of life swept us apart, and when I next sighted him I was clinging to a spar and he was in a well-found boat, which may explain why his nod was rather a perfunctory one. The last time we met, however, was in circumstances which enforced a renewal of our youthful intimacy. It was three or four years ago, and I was returning to Hastings by the midnight train. Getting out at Polegate, for the branch line to Bexhill and Hastings, I perceived Murray, who was also getting out. He saw me, and looked round with a rather desperate air, but Polegate does not present a choice of trains in the early hours of the morning. I greeted him, he nodded, and we got in together. I thought it would be overdoing things to sit opposite him, but from my far corner I told him what pleasure your reproduction of two or three of his stories had given me. There was, I said, one in particular, about Tennyson, which I would very gladly hear again. At once his gloom vanished, and he told the story, superbly. We both roared with laughter, and then, suddenly, he collapsed, staring ahead of him with a blank white face.

There was also, I said, that story about . . . I paused, his face lit up, and another wonderful story came out. Then another collapse. Then another story. And so it went on, until the train, reaching his station, put an end to his misery and to my enjoyment.

Adam's Trade

The next morning Kingsmill said that he would like a day's holiday before starting work, and proposed to spend it in Hastings. 'I am longing to see it all again, after my pinchbeck nomadism of the last fourteen months, but it might be as well if I worked off my nostalgia for the place on my own. I can imagine you getting a little restless after a bit.' His friend approved his insight, but said that before setting off he must have a look at the kitchen-garden, which Pearson had dug due east of the house, and which was now thick with vegetables of all sorts. So they went along to it.

Kingsmill: This is very impressive. You must have worked damned hard to produce this result.

Pearson: Don't you believe it! Digging is a very pleasant, easy, recreational way of passing one's time; and there's nothing like six hours of it to make one feel ten years younger. When I was in the army twenty-five years ago I used to indulge in hard manual labour under every extreme of heat and cold for sixteen hours a day for months on end, and I never felt better in my life. It is the cant of the moment to exalt farming and so on, because it's human to make something noble of necessity. But no one who has done any hard thinking should dignify physical labour with the name of Work. One hour's biography-writing tires me far more than eight hours of road-making or scything or hay-making or white-washing or cinder-shifting or digging or anything else I have done with my hands. Of course three months of continuous manual labour bore me to death, but that's another matter. It doesn't bore a labourer because he knows no better. You may remember that when Beethoven's brother had 'landowner' printed on his cards, Beethoven had 'brainowner' printed on his. He was quite right. Don't waste your admiration on Adam. Keep it for Shakespeare.

Kingsmill: All the same, if Beethoven hadn't felt a twinge of annoyance about his brother being a landowner, he wouldn't have gone to the trouble of asserting his own superiority. The truth is, we all want to be everything, and I regret that I have no manual exploits either in the last war or in this to set against yours.

Why Hens Lay Eggs

They moved on to the poultry department, and stood for a while watching several hens scratching the ground, to the accompaniment of a low crooning sound, which always reminded Pearson of human beings singing love-songs to one another on the wireless.

Pearson: Why do hens lay eggs?

Kingsmill: I see no reason why they shouldn't.

Pearson: Nor I. But that doesn't answer the question: Why do they?

Kingsmill: In my innocent childhood I used to think

it was the result of intercourse with cocks, but on learning that they could lay them as easily without as with cocks, I gave it up.

Pearson: Precisely. They lay them irresponsibly, as a hobby. If they didn't look so damned serious while on the job, I should say they laid them for fun.

Kingsmill: They are women. Whatever their motive, it is a serious one. But am I the first person you have approached on the subject?

Pearson: Good heavens, no! I've button-holed everybody. I'm becoming a public pest. When I appear in the village people smile and shake their heads. 'Here's the fellow,' they probably say, 'who wants to know why hens lay eggs.'

Kingsmill: Can no one advance a plausible reason?

Pearson: No. Most of them seem to think that eggs happen, like rain; that hens lay much as grass grows; that they can't help themselves.

Kingsmill: Is it not possible that hens, habituated to sitting on eggs, find life intolerable with no eggs to sit on, and so, by sheer will power, produce eggs even when their mates, through ennui, malice, a taste for celibacy or any other reason, refuse to co-operate?

Pearson: That sounds all right, but it still doesn't explain why they lay in such unlimited quantities.

Kingsmill: Here again I can come to your rescue. Originally, no doubt, the quantity produced was just enough to provide sitting accommodation. But when human beings began to sneak their cushions, the hens redoubled their efforts. It is the same with cows, who now give far more milk than their calves require. A ceaseless stream of eggs, with or without male assistance, has therefore become second nature with hens. If you have any further problems to lay before me on my return, I shall be happy to consider them.

Our Patron Saint

As he travelled towards Hastings on the Battle bus, Kingsmill was struck by the tranquillity of the Defence Zone, Danger Area, or whatever it was called. There were few people about, and fewer cars; a deep calm seemed to have descended on the cattle in the fields bordering the high ridge along which the bus ran; and when Beachy Head came into view, and he had his first sight of the sea for fourteen months, he felt as though the menace of May 1940 had receded into an infinite distance. Hastings itself was mournful, the barbed wire along the promenade cheerless, and the sight of his untenanted home gave him a disconnected sensation, as though the magnet which had held Hastings together had disappeared, and the whole which he had loved been scattered into unrelated fragments.

Asked on his return how he had enjoyed himself, he indicated that the passage of time, the transiency of sublunary things, and so on, had occupied his thoughts for the greater part of the afternoon. Pearson inclined his head courteously, and they sat down to an excellent meal, after which Kingsmill asked his friend if he had been meditating on the theme of their book.

Pearson replied that he had done more than meditate: he had written a brief life of England's patron saint, St. George, which would give Kingsmill a text to moralize upon, if he felt so disposed. 'A patron saint,' said Pearson, 'should represent the main characteristics of the nation which adopts him; and though I cannot say that George symbolizes what is finest in England, he undoubtedly stands for Big Business, and was a typical City magnate.'

Kingsmill: Gibbon has something about him, hasn't he? He makes him out to have been an army contractor, I believe.

Pearson: Yes, Gibbon is my authority, and I will read you out what I have written:

'George, surnamed the Cappodocian, was born in Cilicia in the fourth century after Judas Iscariot. Starting life in a fuller's shop, he toadied to a number of influential people with such success that he became an army contractor. But a fat commission to supply the troops with bacon was not enough for George. By corrupt and fraudulent means he continued to rake in the shekels until some patriotic citizen, or less successful rascal, brought his actions to the notice of the police. He decamped, but managed to save his fortune by professing Arianism, the fashionable faith of the moment. To prove his zeal he collected a library of books on theology and philosophy, and, being clearly a man who would stop at nothing, read them. This got him into high favour with the dominant religious clique, and he was appointed Archbishop of Alexandria, a post that had recently been held by the exiled Athanasius, the well-known Trinitarian. Our George was hostile to the Trinity. As a follower of Arius he was professedly unitarian in belief; and he was wholeheartedly unitarian in business, the unit being himself. Resuming the commercial career which his theological studies had interrupted, he oppressed both pagans and Christians in his diocese with a fine impartiality. By seizing the monopoly of nitre, salt, paper, funerals and other domestic necessities, he ruined the merchants of Alexandria. He instituted a tax on all the houses, he robbed the temples, and added to his income by playing the part of an informer. Though a man of outstanding business ability, he was too avaricious to be agreeable, and the people rose against him. He fled; but with the help of an armed force he regained his position and revenged himself on those who had driven him forth. The Roman Emperor Constantius died in

A.D. 361, and his successor Julian deposed George. Athanasius returned to wrestle with the Trinity at Alexandria, and George was imprisoned with two of his ministers. Convinced that justice would not be done on him so long as he had a balance at the bank, a pagan mob stormed the prison, murdered George and his associates, slung their bodies over the back of a camel, paraded them through the streets for the entertainment of the citizens, and flung them into the sea.

'The Arians naturally made a martyr of George, and about a century later the Pope made a saint of him. He is perhaps the only purely business man who has been canonized, but then, alas! very few purely business men have been martyred.'

Kingsmill: Gibbon's forebears, one of whom made a fortune in the South Sea Bubble, not being among the few. Gibbon may be right about the historical St. George, and may have been influenced by him, in view of the fact that, although very well off, he secured a sinecure job which brought him in seven or eight hundred a year 'clear'—'clear' meaning that he did nothing of any kind to earn it. But to less erudite Englishmen St. George is a legendary hero, inspired by whom they have made the exertions necessary to keep Englishmen like Gibbon in comfort and security.

As to the historical George, I should like to hear some one else besides Gibbon on him. It is at any rate clear that he took much bigger risks as a theologian than Gibbon as a sceptic.

Pearson: Gibbon appears to jar on you.

Kingsmill: I like the detachment with which in his

autobiography he sums up the varying merits of his six volumes; his serene melancholy over the autumn of his life is moving; and I love the account of the evening when he completed his history, and took a turn or two up and down an avenue of acacias, Lake Leman below him in the calm moonlight. But he bought his irony too cheap, and is, with Jane Austen, the favourite reading of a certain kind of academic prig, who likes to find persons of undoubted genius as preoccupied with cash and comfort as himself.

Joseph and Beatrice

One afternoon, deciding to take a rest from work, Pearson and Kingsmill called for Kitty Muggeridge at the Mill House and accompanied her to the home of her parents, Mr. and Mrs. George Dobbs, who lived on an eminence overlooking one of the most beautiful views in the south of England, a view whose merits Pearson was always impressing on them, when they met, but which they thought little of in comparison with the Swiss mountain scenery they had enjoyed during their long association with the firm of Sir Henry Lunn.

Pearson had been anxious for some time to learn whether there was any truth in the rumour that Mrs. Dobbs's sister, Mrs. Sidney Webb, had in her young days as Beatrice Potter been in love with Joseph Chamberlain. Over tea he disclosed his curiosity on this matter; and

Mrs. Dobbs, after demurring on general grounds to giving a specific answer, and then demurring on specific grounds to giving a general answer, replied that Joseph Chamberlain had certainly been in love with her sister. He used to come and stay at their father's house, and she had often seen Mr. Chamberlain and Beatrice perambulating the grounds, backwards and forwards, and to and fro, oblivious of the world, their heads together in deep argument on social and political questions. Was Beatrice pretty? Kingsmill asked. Extremely, Mrs. Dobbs replied. Was she, asked Kingsmill, in love with Chamberlain? 'I do not know,' said Mrs. Dobbs. 'But Mr. Chamberlain was very autocratic, and all the women round him had to agree with everything he said, and that didn't suit Beatrice, who had very strong views herself. And besides Mr. Chamberlain was old enough to be her father, and had already been married twice, and had two grown-up sons, Austen and Neville.'

Pearson inquired if there had been anything approaching an engagement between them. No, said Mrs. Dobbs; her father had been strongly against the match. However, she added, a reporter, commenting on Mr. Chamberlain's presence at their house parties, had mentioned herself, Miss Rosie Potter, as the magnet that had drawn the great statesman.

On their way back across the fields, Pearson and Kingsmill wondered, rather inconclusively, whether the present state of the world would have been appreciably different if Joseph had married Beatrice, with the possible corollary that Sidney Webb would have married no one, and that Shaw would have married Sidney Webb.

Dickens and Thackeray

They spent a lazy Sunday on August 3rd. After lunch Pearson reclined on a sofa reading *Great Expectations*, and Kingsmill reclined on another sofa reading *The Newcomes*.

'When we were young,' said Kingsmill over tea, 'Dickens and Thackeray were thought to be as firmly fixed in the literary heaven as Homer and Virgil. I suppose it was due to the Victorian feeling that their age was the crown and culmination of history, and that Dickens and Thackeray, Tennyson and Browning, Macaulay and Carlyle, had between them rounded literature off.

> *Pearson:* And nowadays Thackeray is completely blown up, and Dickens is being contested in a rearguard action.

> *Kingsmill:* I used to love *The Newcomes*, and looking at it now brings back the emotions of those days. It is full of Thackeray's nostalgia for his youth, and when I read it at the age of thirteen his retrospective regret seemed to be mine too, and I shared his longing for a sunny time now gone for ever, vaguely thought of as a period when barouches bowled by, with demure young damsels and severe matrons inside, and young men roamed a leisurely Europe, making innocent love to flaxen-haired girls along the Rhine, and revelling in the gay open-air life of France, with its funny little soldiers marching along in their red breeches.

> *Pearson:* Dickens was the creator of London to me,

and when I arrived there I spent a lot of time in searching round corners for his characters. But there is nothing of my own early years in Dickens, and in re-reading *David Copperfield* lately, although I think the first quarter of it the best bit of writing in English fiction, I never felt I was out of fairyland.

Kingsmill: I still, at odd moments, when I'm walking in London, see corners of houses, or name-boards over shops, or a leaning lamp-post, as though they belonged to the London of Dickens and Phiz. Only a momentary impression, but leaving behind a sense of regret, utterly different from that left by Thackeray. The world of Thackeray is one which you have lost, Dickens's one which you have never found.

Big Gangsters

One morning at breakfast, Pearson, never at his most benevolent at that time, flung down the paper, at which he had been giving a cursory and unfriendly glance. Asked by Kingsmill what particular item had been too much for him, he replied that if one thing sickened him more than another at the moment, which was doubtful, it was the attempt of the Communists to pretend that the national resistance of Russia sprang from an international enthusiasm for that bearded imbecile, Karl Marx. The mass of Englishmen, he went on, had no use for dictatorships, but in the last twenty years there were four sections of the nation which had been gulled by the prevailing insanity in Russia, Germany, Italy and Turkey. After the Russo-German pact and the outbreak of war, they had, all four of them, executed a rapid retreat, but in their hearts they were still totalitarian, still hoped to convert England into a slave state, and those of them who favoured the Communist brand were now perking up again.

Kingsmill: The four sections being . . . ?

Pearson: Recruited from the working classes, the plutocracy, the Roman Catholics and the aristocracy. The last three complained of the communism of the first, but you and I needn't go into that, for we have known all along that the only difference between the Nazis, the Fascists and the Communists is in the name: they all cringe to the State, and want to create a nation of serfs.

Of course we can sympathize with the resentment of the poor, which is all that Communism in this country ever amounted to, but we can only view with disgust the snobbery and stupidity of the rich, who, not content with their dividends, would bully and browbeat and enslave still further those who sweat so that they may be content to be snobbish and stupid. I beg your pardon?

Kingsmill: Granted. I was only clearing my throat.

Pearson: I am staggered by the imbecility of so many men who still pass for intelligent. The average out-and-out supporter of Hitler or Mussolini was, of course, either a fool or a blackguard.

Kingsmill: I notice that they are now saying they were fools, not blackguards, and softening this admission still further by claiming that every one else was a fool too.

Pearson: But what is one to say when some one as shrewd as Shaw is taken in by these dictators? He was quite favourably disposed towards Hitler and Mussolini, and was an all-in Stalinite. While I was writing his Life, I had an argument with him about the model of all dictators, Julius Caesar. I said that Shakespeare's Julius was obviously the right conception of the character because we had lived to see his doubles in Europe to-day. Shaw scoffed at Shakespeare's dictator as a caricature, having in one of his plays conceived Caesar as a tolerant and humorous humanitarian, very much like himself. He maintained that his was the right, and Shakespeare's the wrong, portrait of a dictator. But the outbreak of the war placed him in rather a ticklish position. So in an article for *Time and Tide*, written long after our argument, he tried to get out of the difficulty by referring to Julius Caesar as an 'adventurer, explorer, soldier, demagogue and what-not (gangster if you like)', and went on to lump him in with the others as follows: 'In judging Julius Caesar, Cromwell, Napoleon, Mussolini, Hitler and the rest, we must bear in mind that they all tried democracy and found it could not even keep them out of prison.'

On seeing this I dropped him a line reminding him that precisely the same thing could be said of Charles Peace, Crippen, Landru, Burke, Hare, and all the totalitarians who were doing seven-year stretches on Dartmoor.

Kingsmill: Did he reply?

Pearson: No. The outstanding fact about these dictators is that they are still boys; they have never got beyond the age of twelve; they are precisely what I was at that age.

Little Gangsters

Kingsmill: Precisely?

Pearson: Precisely. In the days of my youth grown-up people used to talk of original sin. What they meant was that they perceived their own early characteristics reappearing in their children, and were so furious at the reminder that they fell back upon the wisdom of that pompous old ass Solomon, and reached for the nearest rod. I was full of original sin, and the evil of my mind was duly scored upon my behind.

My sins consisted of raiding strawberry beds and peach trees (Lebensraum), insulting tradesmen (Goebbels on the pluto-democracies), laying traps for passing pedestrians and watching them sprawling on their faces (Schuschnigg at Berchtesgaden), throwing stones at birds, cats, dogs and other mobile objects (dive-bombing refugees), and a multitude of similar diversions, all coming under one or other of the above categories—such as puncturing bicycle tyres, locking up my elders in bedrooms, lighting bonfires, climbing trees, crawling over roofs, swarming up the sides of houses—and then manfully lying about it all.

When I was a day-boy at a private school in Bedford I was always getting into trouble. A lad named Rex Tetley formed the other partner in the Axis, and our special victim was an old gentleman who lived at the top of Waldeck Avenue and did not like having his front-door bell rung for our amusement. We objected to his face; we particularly resented his beard; and we took exception to his clothes. So every evening, at 5.45 p.m., on our way home from school we rang his front-door bell, and passed quickly on.

Like England, he took some rousing, but suddenly one evening he appeared from behind a privet bush, cutting off our retreat. He asked us why we had rung his bell. We had no adequate explanation to offer. Whereat he boxed our ears unmercifully, knocked our heads together, and sent us on our way with dire threats of what would happen to us if we did not change our habits.

One dark winter evening, about ten days later, we stood in the road outside his house with several large and jagged stones in our hands. At a given signal we hurled two of them with all our force at his dining-room window. Crash! Satisfied, we dropped the rest of our ammunition, and were off. But beard-face was out of his house and in full cry before we got to the end of the road. Into my garden we went, and the net result of the matter was that my father had to pay for a brand-new plate-glass window, and I had to pay for his payment across his knee.

Then there was the milkman. There was a sort of moral vindictiveness in his expression which I did not like. He was an earnest milkman. He took his job seriously. He never made that cheerful note on the top register which most milkmen make. So, having recently acquired an airgun, I loaded it with slug, and lay in wait for him. Down the road he came, in gaiters, his red walrus moustache looking more revolting than ever. When he got level with the house, I leant out of my bedroom window, took careful aim, and fired. The slug penetrated his clothing, and clearly gave him a pang. This sent me into fits of laughter, and the upshot of the downshot was an interview between the milkman and my father, and another interview between my father and me.

I am glad that children nowadays have other ways of passing the time. At my time of life I should not care to get a stone in the back of my neck as I strolled down the street; I want no bricks through my windows, and no foreign substances dropped in my milk by sportive schoolboys on their way to an early morning swim. That is why I dislike dictators, who fling bombs about as I used to fling stones, take violent dislikes to harmless people, and cut down our rations as I used to steal or dilute them. But what about doing a bit of work?

Kingsmill: One moment. Your implied assumption that my early years were contemplative, not active, is, in the main, true. Like the Duke in *Measure for Measure* I have ever loved the life removed, but as my brother Arnold was of a more stirring type I often found myself bearing a hand of sorts in his amusements. One sport of his would have appealed to you. It consisted in rolling down the mountain-side the large stones collected in cairns by Swiss cowherds. Grass at high altitudes is not, at the best, very nourishing, and of course if it is overlaid by large stones it isn't at its best, even if the cows can get at it. Hence these cairns. On several occasions, as we were dispersing cairns, cowherds came panting up, red, wrathful and menacing. The land in these uplands belonged to a mysterious entity called the Commune, and as the cowherds rushed upon us, we used to cry out: 'Touch us, and we will tell the Commune,' at which their hands fell to their sides, and, like baffled ogres, they would slink away, why I have never since been able to discover.

Pearson: Extraordinary. And now, I think, we really ought to adjourn for the business of the day.

Kingsmill: Though, as I have said, of a contemplative nature, I was not so contemplative as to feel any twinge of remorse as they receded, muttering. It so happens that I can measure the growth of my moral nature with some exactitude by comparing with my insensibility at twelve the agony I went through at thirty-three, on the occasion of inadvertently rolling some rocks down a mountain-side above the Lake of Lucerne.

Pearson: I shall be delighted to hear all about it this evening.

Kingsmill: Your pipe needs refilling, and my story is a short one. One day when I was in my Lucerne office one of our tourists came in, a stout middle-aged woman. She had just returned from the

Burgenstock, she told me, and had dropped her bag down the precipice at the top. It contained her passport, a spare set of false teeth, and twenty-five pounds in English notes. It was a most serious loss, and could I possibly do anything about it?

I went to the Burgenstock the next afternoon, and decided to scramble down where the ground was less precipitous, and work round to the bottom of the cliff. The place I chose for my descent, though not at all sheer, was fairly steep, and the loose stones I dislodged bounded out of sight in four or five leaps. Suddenly, just after I had dislodged two or three small rocks, I heard piercing shrieks from below. It at once came back to me that there was a path, much frequented by sight-seers, three hundred feet or so below me; and that I had knocked out at least one sightseer seemed to me, from the agony in the screams, almost a certainty. Pulling myself together, I went on descending, feeling that the least I could do would be to collect any farewell messages. At once I started another rock or two off, and a second later still more agonizing shrieks came up to me. Was I pounding out my victim's last breath? Collecting myself again, and drawing a deep breath, I proceeded, with extreme gingerliness. The path came into my view, to my right, about fifty yards away, and three young girls were standing on it, white and shaking. I hurried towards them, and one, shorter and more formidable than her companions, began to upbraid me bitterly. Melted at last by my apologies, she explained what had happened. They had been sitting on a bench, a little way down the path, and were about to rise when my first consignment of rocks shot above their heads, missing them by a yard or so, cleared the path, and vanished. This was when they shrieked first. Then, just when they had summoned courage to make a dash for it, the second lot shot over their heads—and more shrieks.

We made friends; they were working-girls from French Switzerland; I took them to the Burgenstock hotel for tea, and sent them on the Rhone Glacier Motor Tour the next day. On a card I had from them on their return they wrote: '*Le temps était splendide, la compagnie charmante, et bien sûr que cette journée du 21 août 1923 n'a pas compté de petites filles plus heureuses que nous.*' Their names were Betty, Lily and Alice. Funny to think they must be nearly forty by now.

Pearson: What about the false teeth, passport and loose notes?

Kingsmill: A chap went down the cliff on a rope and got them. Might almost be grandmothers by now. . . . Well, there you are.

The Church of England

On the second Sunday of Kingsmill's visit, the two friends set off for Burwash, walking to Mountfield, a wayside station, where they waited for the train to Etchingham. They got their tickets from the caretaker of the station, whose occupations were manifold, seeming to include opening and shutting the gates at the level crossings, spraying the insects on his rambler roses, dusting his hens, and keeping an eye open for stray passengers.

Sitting on the rustic platform, they agreed that a rural landscape without a railway running through it wasn't a rural landscape.

Kingsmill: Ruskin missed this truth because there weren't any railways in his childhood, and so he had never watched railway lines converging peacefully in the distance between green banks and dwindling telegraph poles.

Pearson: One must therefore admit that the children of the present age will in middle life view pylons, aeroplanes and the other modern blights with romantic and favourable eyes.

They left the train at Etchingham and as they walked past the church heard the strains of the organ. Entering the churchyard they stood for some time by the porch listening to the service.

Pearson was much struck by two phrases which he had never noticed when he used to hear them Sunday after Sunday in his youth: 'O Lord, make clean our hearts within us'—'And take not thy holy spirit from us.' They were walking away and he had begun to praise the Litany when the congregation started to sing the Old Hundredth. They paused to listen.

'Isn't it extraordinary,' said Pearson, as they left the churchyard, 'how utterly unmoved by all this I was in my youth? I suppose it's because one never appreciates a thing until one can see it at a distance.'

Kingsmill: And when the heart is just beginning to beat faster, it doesn't want to be overhauled. A girl singing a few pews away means more to one than the Holy Spirit. Hence much trouble over many years.

Pearson: At the end of which one wants to get back to one's pew, and give the Holy Spirit a chance.

Kingsmill: Should he still be willing to take it.

Pearson: Why is it that the Church of England is so much more poetic than any other church?

Kingsmill: Probably because the Protestant churches, Lutheran, Baptist, Wesleyan, and so on, set out to get into direct contact with God, and the Catholic Church pushes God completely into the background.

Pearson: Whereas the English Church, by keeping the old ritual but putting it in the mother tongue, leaves it to each individual worshipper to sample as much of the divine as suits him.

Kingsmill: An arrangement propitious to poetic feeling.

Thomas Cranmer

Pearson: I suppose one may call the English Prayer Book the best-known prose work in the language. It has certainly kept the Church of England going, which proves once more that art has a more permanent effect on the minds of men than religion. Yet how few people know the name of the author of the only prose work we all know by heart!

Kingsmill: Few indeed! Who is he?

Pearson: Thomas Cranmer.

Kingsmill: Did he write the whole Prayer Book?

Pearson: All the best things in it—the Litany, and nearly all the finest prayers.

Kingsmill: Then he must have been a real genius. I know that he helped Henry VIII with his divorces, and thrust his right hand into the fire when he was burnt by Queen Mary. But that's all I do know.

Pearson: 'Nothing in his life became him like the leaving it.'

Kingsmill: Was the rest of his life unbecoming, his prose apart?

Pearson: Pretty shady. He was dragged into public affairs, rather reluctantly, over the divorce of Katharine, and he owed his rise to power largely to Anne Boleyn, whose life he later swore away to save his own. As Archbishop of Canterbury, he was simply Henry's tool, doing whatever the King wanted him to do. He never hesitated to perjure himself. He regularly officiated at the

Mass, which he thought idolatrous. He betrayed to death another of Henry's wives, Catherine Howard. Most of the religious leaders in that age were content to burn those with whom they disagreed. Cranmer burnt those with whom he agreed. This he did to oblige Henry, who remained a Catholic all his life, and therefore required his Archbishop to proceed against anti-Catholics, the most convinced of whom was Cranmer himself. No wonder he laid such stress on 'miserable sinners' in the wonderful Litany he wrote for the Prayer Book.

Kingsmill: Any light in the picture?

Pearson: Yes. He had no interest in money, which at a time when every gangster in the country was plundering the Church may be regarded as exceptional virtue. Though socially dull, he was easy to get on with, courteous, suave and mild, and his crimes were the effect of caution, not cruelty. It may also be urged in his favour that he was a sensualist. At least his love-affairs prove that he was human.

Kingsmill: How many did he have?

Pearson: Dozens, if his expression is any guide. Two are known to history. When at Cambridge he forfeited his fellowship at Jesus College by marrying an inn-keeper's daughter, a local wench known as Black Joan. She died in childbirth, and he got his fellowship back again. Later he took a serious risk, which in view of his timid nature shows how susceptible he was. When middle-aged he went to Germany on a delicate diplomatic mission, and married a girl young enough to be his daughter. If his marriage had become known he would have been ruined, because he was then a Catholic priest, and Henry had not broken away from Rome. The story goes that he had the second Mrs. Cranmer brought over to England in a tub. Safely here, he kept her hidden, presumably not in the tub. But even the Catholics cannot deny that he made a good end. He steadily held out into the flames the hand that had written those recantations which he hoped would save

him from the stake, but which he loathed and despised in his heart; and he died without a murmur.

Kingsmill: Poor Cranmer—something really great in him, in spite of everything. No wonder his prayers are so fine, the appeals of some one who believed in God and goodness, and longed for deliverance. People excuse the uninspired prayers turned out by Anglicans nowadays on the ground that modern prose does not give them a chance. If they had anything to say, modern prose would serve them as well as the prose of any other age.

A deprecating attitude towards science does not produce great devotional literature. Since the middle of last century most of the leading figures in the Church of England have been secretly convinced that Darwin said the last word on the universe, their only regret being that he did not say it in such a form that a well-endowed church could be built up round it.

Burwash

The road from Etchingham, long, straight and dull for a good part of the way, became prettier as they approached Burwash, and as they entered the main street of the village they were amazed by the beauty of the place, the old church, a Jacobean mansion or two, and a row of houses with a pavement lined by trees recalling the Pantiles at Tunbridge Wells on a smaller but more exquisite scale.

Pearson: How is it that no one has told us that Burwash is one of the loveliest villages in England?

Kingsmill: I had no idea it would be like this. One had heard the name, which rather suggests a pigsty. But this is as beautiful as anything I have seen since Bibury.

In their bemused ecstasy they passed an inn which offered them the lunch they were by this time in need of, and went on to the end of the street, where they became conscious of a public house called The Bear.

Taking their drinks into the garden at the back, they sat there for a while, enjoying a pleasant view.

Having been apprised by the landlord of The Bear that no one in Burwash would be able to provide them with food of any kind whatsoever, they went to the Bell Inn, where they had an excellent lunch. Afterwards, as they sat in the lounge, discussing Mahomet and Hitler, an old lady in an arm-chair rose with a frown, and having ferreted round in the interstices of the chair, to make sure that she had left no belonging of any value, went out of the room. Pausing a moment to wonder that an opportunity of overhearing their conversation should be sacrificed, Pearson and Kingsmill resumed their discussion.

From The Bell they went down the road to call on Kingsmill's brother, Brian Lunn, with whom they had tea. Kingsmill having mentioned the Stratford-on-Avon Preservation Committee, Brian recalled that at about the time their father had been doing his best to preserve Stratford for the English nation, he had also been doing his best to retrieve Santa Sofia for Christendom.

'Everything was going along quite all right,' said Brian, in his slow voice. 'None of the bishops on the committee minded Santa Sofia being Christian again, and the Foreign Office was quite in favour of the idea, and as the Turks weren't in a position to do anything about it in 1919, everything would have been fixed if it hadn't been for Rome.'

'Rome?' queried Pearson.

'The Catholics didn't want the Greek Church to have the oldest and biggest cathedral in Christendom, so they pulled strings, and the whole thing fell through.'

Brian, promising to put them on to a short cut which would save them the trudge along the main road to Etchingham, led them along ravines, and over streams, and through undergrowth, until eventually they joined the Etchingham road just outside Burwash.

Thomas Gray

A bus came up with them, and they took it to Hurst Green, where, the conductor told them, they could pick up another bus, which would get them to Battle by seven. Dismounting at Hurst Green, they stood dubiously on the pavement, jostled by pedestrians, and wondering how they would pass the next hour and a half. On a sudden impulse, they rushed after the bus, which was bound for Hawkhurst, scrambled on to it, and up the stairs. Surprised to see them so soon again, the conductor said 'Has some one lost you?' and at Hawkhurst, when they got off, he called to them 'Sure you're quite safe?'

On the way to Hawkhurst, Kingsmill pointed to a gate leading into a field, and said: 'I think that must be the very gate I saw a young man leaning on six years ago. I was walking from Hawkhurst to Etchingham; it was a summer evening, and he was gazing at the setting sun. It was just like a picture, and brought to my mind that quatrain which Gray later omitted from his Elegy, and which I think is the most beautiful in the poem:

'"Him have we seen the greenwood side along,
    While o'er the heath we hied, our labour done,
    What time the woodlark piped her farewell song,
    With wistful eyes pursue the setting sun."'

Pearson: I think an even more beautiful quatrain, also
    cut by Gray from the final version, is:

'There, scattered oft, the earliest of the year,
    By hands unseen, are showers of violets found,
    The redbreast loves to build and warble there,
    And little footsteps lightly print the ground.'

Kingsmill: And then there's that other lovely verse
    he cancelled:

'Hark, how the sacred calm that breathes around
    Bids every fierce tumultuous passion cease,
    In still small accents whispering from the ground
    A grateful earnest of eternal peace.'

Isn't it incredible, or rather wouldn't it be incredible if Gray hadn't been a don, that a man capable of writing such exquisite poetry should be so shocked on seeing it again as to hurry it out of sight, like a woman removing a slop-pail from the hall when the front-door bell rings?

Pearson: How wonderfully English the *Elegy* is, and how entirely the little church becomes a part of the landscape, without obtruding its special function. 'Yonder ivy-mantled tower'—the Church of England in all its ample repose.

Kingsmill: It's interesting that the most popular poems in our language were all written by recluses, who knew nothing about ordinary life, either in its details or its responsibilities—Gray's *Elegy*, Fitz-Gerald's *Omar*, and Housman's *Shropshire Lad*—all the work of cloistered celibates.

Pearson: That's one way of putting it. And you can add Tennyson's *In Memoriam* to your list, although Tennyson had bushier whiskers than was suspected by the critic who wrote that *In Memoriam* must have come from the full heart of the widow of a military man.

Kingsmill: I suppose it's because the permanent mood of these recluses is dissatisfaction with life that they have been able to give such appealing expression to the intermittent dissatisfaction of ordinary people.

Hawkhurst

'Hawkhurst,' said Kingsmill, as they waved to the bus conductor, 'is associated for me with the Bishop of London—not the present one, but Winnington Ingram. I came here once or twice in 1935 to put in a few hours on a biography of Winnington Ingram which a friend of mine, Percy Colson, had embarked upon. Colson, who was in the sixties, preferred reading to writing, conversation to reading, the social round to conversation, and six thousand a year to the complications of ecclesiastical biography. The period in his life when he had had six thousand a year was long past, the business of keeping afloat was not becoming any easier as time went on, and he was much pleased when the Bishop of London, for whom by the way he had a real affection, expressed his willingness to be written about. It was easy to get a book on so popular a figure commissioned, and in the first glow of half the advance on signature of contract Colson, who used occasionally to look in on me at Hastings, recaptured the zest for life which was fast slipping from him. His period, as he often told me, was the nineties, not the nineties of Kipling, still less of Cecil Rhodes, but of Wilde and Beardsley and Ernest Dowson —paganism softened by Catholic sentiment, and Catholic sentiment strengthened by paganism. And with a solid cheque in the bank that period did not seem quite so irrecoverably vanished as before.

'Colson loved music; the choir of the Middle Temple was one of his greatest delights; and if a life of Winnington Ingram could have been plausibly converted into an essay on church music, Colson would have had nothing to complain about. But it couldn't. Masses of material, dealing with the innumerable activities of his tireless subject, poured in on him, and touched by his agony, and hoping, with little reason as it turned out, that any help I gave him would not prove unduly disinterested, I lent him a hand, and between us we produced a passable book. The Bishop was pleased, the publisher was satisfied, and a fair proportion of the Bishop's countless admirers asked for it at the libraries. If I have not been as kind as I might have been to Dickens, Kipling and one or two others, I hope it will be remembered to my credit that such passages as I interpolated in Colson's life of the Bishop were steeped in loving-kindness.

'Colson must be nearly seventy now, and I was very glad to get a letter from him only a week or two ago, telling me that he had come to rest in the hospital of St. Cross at Winchester. He has delightful quarters there, he says; he adores the cathedral and the music; and there are friends in the neighbourhood who connect him, through bridge and pleasant talk, with the social delights of earlier years. It is comforting to hear of such harbours in this stormy world, and as part-biographer of the Bishop of London I, too, perhaps may one day be admitted as a Brother of St. Cross.'

While Kingsmill was talking, Pearson was looking about him to see whether his friend had been justified in claiming that Hawkhurst was as beautiful as Burwash. He decided that it was not, and after they had walked the whole length of the main street Kingsmill withdrew his claim. 'It was perhaps that walk from here to Etchingham, which has made my memory of this place so delightful,' he suggested. 'A perfect summer evening—I shall never forget it.' Pearson forbearing to analyse this defence, they went into a tea-shop, revived themselves with coffee, and returned home by bus.

Pubs

The next day, August 11th, after working till late in the afternoon, Pearson and Kingsmill strolled over the fields to the Royal Oak in Whatlington. Settling

down over their whiskies in the small sitting-room at the back, from which they had a pleasant view of a mass of pink and purple asters in the garden of the inn, they yielded themselves, Pearson to speech and Kingsmill to silence. Pearson's theme was the public house as the only democratic institution in the country. Here a man was at ease with his fellow-beings; here a man could speak freely and be freely interrupted; here alone were men equal; here assembled all the finer spirits in the country-side; here were to be found the chief qualities in the English race, humour and good humour; and only here the greatest imaginative character in English literature and the greatest actual character in English history, Falstaff and Dr. Johnson, were quite at home.

Freely interrupting his friend, Kingsmill, drawing out his note-book, said: 'Before I forget, I have here, noted down for your benefit, three opinions on Falstaff by boys at Merchant Taylors. I asked them to let me know what they thought of King Henry's rejection of Falstaff, and one of them wrote: "I would have pensioned Falstaff off and given him a country house, for old times sake, and told him to lead a comparatively quiet life." A kindly reasonable suggestion, and the "comparatively" shows that the boy understood Falstaff. My second opinion is more hard-boiled: "Had that gentleman left Henry alone, all would have gone smoothly, but it was obvious that even if the king had no more to do with Falstaff and his friends, Falstaff and his friends would have more to do with him." My third opinion is from a very surprising angle. I have discovered that boys manage to combine a feeling that grown-ups are blithering idiots with a touching belief in their superior virtue. They expect an extremely high standard of conduct in their elders, and have no eye for extenuating circumstances. To my third boy Falstaff was simply a disgusting old rascal, and he wrote: "If I had been Prince Hal I would certainly not have treated him in the way that he did. I would have thrown him into prison at once."'

Pearson: Interesting. But where was I? Ah, yes. The humour in pubs varies greatly, but all forms are to be enjoyed. Farmers have a picturesque humour of their own. At the Feathers in Ludlow I heard one of them describe how he had shot at several rabbits that day and had failed to bag

them. 'Plenty o' room round 'em, ain't there?'
said another. But country people have a lot of
time on their hands for solitary brooding, with the
result that, once they get going, they easily become
the world's leading non-stop talkers; and they are
liable to record episodes the comedy in which
may not appeal to outsiders. For example, I heard
the following account of a dialogue the other day,
which stuck in my mind because of the gusto with
which it was told and the hilarity with which it
was received:

''Ow's your turnips?' ses ee. ''Ow's my
turnips?' ses I. 'Yes,' ses ee, ''ow's your turnips?'
'Well,' ses I, 'come to that, 'ow's yourn?'
''Ow's mine?' ses ee. 'Yes,' ses I, ''ow's yourn?'
'Oh,' ses ee, 'they beant too bad.' 'No more,' ses
I, 'ain't mine.' (Laughter.) 'No more ain't
mine,' ses I. (More laughter.)

The loudest shout of mirth I ever heard in a
pub greeted a tale told by a poacher, who in the
course of his nightly prowling had come across
a gamekeeper lying on the ground in a pool of
blood, the victim of an accident. 'Was ee dead?'
asked a yokel during the thrilled hush that fell
upon the company at the bar. 'Dead!' echoed the
poacher: 'Ee'd blown 'is bloody 'ed off! Laff? I
thought I should ha' died o' laffin'!'

Hildenborough

On August 13th Pearson and Kingsmill, who had been invited by Mr. and Mrs. Alan White to spend a night at Hildenborough, took the train there, and were met on the platform by Alan. He was breathing rather heavily, and explained that, the local car not having turned up, he had run most of the way from his house, which was about a mile from the station. While waiting for the car, they sat on a bench admiring the flower-beds with which the station master had beautified the platform, and disagreeing about the artistic merits of the posters. After about ten minutes, Alan asked the station master if he had seen the car. The station master replying that he had, but that it was there no longer, Alan, striking his forehead with his hand, exclaimed: 'That person who got out with you must have taken it.' Pearson proposed that they should walk, and Alan, after expressing his dismay at the horrors into which he had betrayed his guests, at length agreed. They set off, and reached their destination, Nizel's Oast, about twenty minutes later in reasonably good repair.

'This is a wonderful place, Hesketh,' said Kingsmill, as Mrs. White greeted them. 'Make yourself at home. I only wish I could, permanently.'

After dinner Kingsmill said to Alan: 'Well, my optimism about the war is being justified. The Russians are nearing their eighth week, and no one expected them to last more than three.'

Pearson: With the single exception of Bernard Shaw.

White: I'm always glad to meet any one who is

optimistic. Up in London no one seems very cheerful, though of course we are all glad the bombing is over for the time being.

Pearson: What sickens me about the English is, that though the most conceited nation in the world, they always jump at the first opportunity to disparage their own amazing feats. Here are we, who two years ago would have had to be polite to Portugal, and in the last twelve months have with one hand shattered the mightiest armada ever launched against us, and with the other cleaned up our blasted cities. We have beaten every transport record in history by removing the Italian armies in North Africa from behind their front lines to behind our rear ones; we have cleared the oceans for our goods and armies; we have blocked all the efforts of the French to pull us into the mire in which they are wallowing; and in short we have knocked hell out of allies and enemies alike—and yet now, when Russia, who has been dithering behind her steel ramparts all through this, and performing feats of appeasement which would have made Neville Chamberlain blush, is at last attacked, the cry goes up from us: 'What are we doing for this gallant people? Are we to stand idly by while these architects of a new world are fighting hammer and sickle to make a Better Britain possible?'

White: I like to hear you talk like that.

Kingsmill: He likes it himself.

White: Of course we've done wonderfully, but I can't see any reason to assume that Germany is on the downgrade.

Kingsmill: The Germans are so romantic about war that they are bound to lose, unless they win very quickly. In the first heat of a war they can still believe that they are in the middle of a Wagner Opera, but after a year or so it begins to dawn on them that blood and lice and bits of scrap iron raining on them, and synthetic bread and genuine dead horse, aren't the right stage properties for a satisfactory performance of *Siegfried*.

The English on the other hand dislike the idea

of war so heartily that they find the reality quite bearable in comparison with what they had expected. If the Germans ever learn to relax between wars, they may possibly avoid going to bits during them.

White: I don't see any signs of them going to bits yet.

The talk passed to books, and Alan regaled them with many stories from his own experience as a publisher, the general effect of which was to convince Pearson and Kingsmill that publishers, too, had their crosses to bear, the crosses not infrequently being authors.

On the following morning Pearson, hearing that

Penshurst, the home of Sir Philip Sidney, was only five miles away, set off to revisit it. On the way he passed through a village, from the church in which emerged a kindly white-haired clergyman. Pearson asked him the way to Penshurst, and after directing him the clergyman said:

'Surely I know you?'

'I don't think so.'

'Your face is familiar to me.'

'Doubtless there are many like it.'

'You do yourself an injustice. May I ask your name?'

'Hesketh Pearson.'

'Not the author of my favourite book?'

'I cannot claim to have written the Bible.'

'Ah, that's different. I mean the Life of Sydney Smith.'

Pearson, pleased by this encouraging encounter, inquired how the clergyman had come to recognize him, learnt that it was from a photograph in his reminiscences, and shaking hands cordially proceeded on his way to Penshurst, whence, after a drink at the Leicester Arms, he returned home at the rate of five miles an hour.

After an agreeable afternoon in the garden, Pearson and Kingsmill said farewell, got into the local car, which had recovered from its capricious humour of the previous day, and drove to the station.

When One Would Like to Have Lived

'A delightful station,' said Kingsmill, looking at the flower-beds, as the train got under way. 'I find that many boys are under the illusion that it must have been romantic to travel by stage-coach. I used to think so myself; but, even assuming that the landlord came out to welcome one in from the darkness, had a sirloin of beef ready, and didn't overcharge one, that would not make up for the cold and boredom of the long slow journey, the congested accommodation, the lurching in and out of ruts, the difficulty of reading and the low general average of the conversation. On the whole I prefer this age to any other, especially now that there are less cars about.'

Pearson: I prefer it to any other without qualification, as I would rather be alive than dead. Also a man who has really been alive in his own age would rather have been alive in his own age.

Kingsmill: But if you would rather be dead than alive, which of past ages would you choose to have lived, and died, in?

Pearson: To any one who, like myself, is primarily interested in the things of the spirit, there can be but one reply. Allowing me the biblical span of three-score-years-and-ten, I should like to have been born in 1765.

Kingsmill: Then you would have known Johnson when you were just old enough to appreciate him. . . .

Pearson: And Dickens and Thackeray when they were just old enough to be appreciated.

Kingsmill: There have certainly never been so many

good poets as during that seventy years—Wordsworth, Blake, Burns, Goethe, Keats, Shelley, Heine, Hugo, Coleridge and Tennyson.

Pearson: And nearly all the greatest musicians: Beethoven, Mozart, Haydn and Schubert.

Kingsmill: The unique combination of Johnson and Boswell.

Pearson: The best English artists: Constable, Turner and Rowlandson.

Kingsmill: And essayists: Hazlitt and Lamb.

Pearson: Walter Scott.

Kingsmill: Carlyle.

Pearson: Sydney Smith.

Kingsmill: Sheridan.

Pearson: And for those who relish action, Nelson and Wellington.

Kingsmill: And for those who relish acting, Kean, Byron and Napoleon.

Pearson: In fact, the period includes every remarkable man one would like to have seen or met, except Shakespeare, who, to be frank, I would rather have seen or met than all the others put together.

Kingsmill: On the subject of Shakespeare you are a religious fanatic.

Pearson: A love of Shakespeare is incompatible with religion or fanaticism. But I see what you mean.

First Love

Michael, Brian Lunn's son, who had come to Wood. Place for a few days in order to be near the young Muggeridges, afforded occasional matter for retrospective reflection to Pearson and Kingsmill. At supper one evening, with the insouciance of thirteen, he indicated that young girls were apt to be rather a nuisance. They got sentimental, and interfered with things. He instanced a very pretty little girl whom he had met on a previous visit.

'That kid whom Michael referred to at supper,' Kingsmill said to Pearson as they were smoking afterwards, 'was really lovely. In three or four years time, he'd give his ears for a kind word from her, and would get nothing but kicks. Another five or six years, and the situation might be reversed again, with the girl ready to marry and Michael deciding that forty is quite early enough to think about settling down.'

Pearson: I had reached the advanced age of eighteen before I fell in love. One has lots of flirtations with girls in one's later teens, and in my own case they are so confused that I cannot pick one from t'other. And one has lots of odd memories which are like so many glimpses of love before it is aroused. I can still see the face and figure of a girl coming down the stairs of a London hotel where I was staying as a boy.

Kingsmill: I remember when I was ten a beautiful woman, in the late twenties, I think, pausing on the stairs of a Swiss hotel, and giving me her hand with a smile which rewarded me for having looked at her for some days with hopeless longing across the dining-room.

Pearson: But, I repeat, I was eighteen before I really fell in love. The object of my passion, which I naturally considered the most tremendous emotional upheaval that had ever happened to any one since the beginning of the world, was an actress. She was, I need hardly say, the loveliest woman who ever lived. She had, I need scarcely add, the most angelic features, the most exquisite shape, the most graceful movements and the most divine voice ever possessed by a human being. And of course she was the greatest actress in recorded time. Her name was Evelyn Millard. When I first saw her she was playing the leading female part in a play called *Monsieur Beaucaire*. The chief male part was acted by Lewis Waller, whom I disliked on sight. To my chagrin she stuck to the brute, and I had the pain of seeing him making love to her night after night. I remember feeling greatly relieved on hearing that there was a Mrs. Lewis Waller, and that she was not Evelyn Millard, which seemed to make his behaviour on the stage just bearable, if in bad taste; but I never began to appreciate him as an actor until he had changed his leading lady.

Though I was faithless to Evelyn now and then in a mundane way, my ideal passion for her lasted two years. I wrote love-letters to her, disguised as laudations of her acting; I sent flowers to her; I always led the applause when she made her first appearance in the play; I waited at stage-doors to see her go in or come out; my bedroom walls were covered with photos of her in various parts; I carried picture-postcards of her in my pocket-book; I sent letters to the newspapers about her marvellous performances (never published); I talked about her to every one who could stand it until they could no longer stand it; I found out where she lived and went long distances out of my way in order to pass her house. Sometimes she sent me little courteous notes in reply to my reams, and these accompanied me by day and lay under my pillow at night. After enduring my passion-barrage for nearly two years, she capitulated. That is to say, she decided to see me. I presumed my latest letter had touched her heart, and I was in ecstasies.

She was then at the Lyric Theatre. Her note arrived on a Tuesday morning, and asked me to come round to her dressing-room after the performance on the following Friday, if I would like to. Like to!

During those four days I was conscious of nothing in the universe except that I was going to see her. Friday came. I watched the play in a dream. The curtain fell on the last act. As a rule I stayed on applauding her until I was left in a minority of one and the house-lights went up. But on this occasion I was out of the theatre before the company had taken a call, and was through the stage-door inquiring for Miss Millard while the audience were still applauding.

At the last moment I suffered a frightful spasm of nerves and could hardly enter her room when I was announced. All the pretty speeches I had been preparing stuck in my throat, and after taking her hand I sat on a sofa tongue-tied. She was incredibly sweet to me. But she spoke to me like a mother, and I was cured of my two-years passion in something under ten minutes.

Kingsmill: And what did you feel like on reaching home?

Pearson: Very blue indeed. The world seemed completely empty.

Kingsmill: I suppose by force of contrast I am reminded of a story which, to put it mildly, lacks the poetry and idealism of yours.

Service not Self

Some years ago a minor official called on me one day from some firm. I forget what about, only remembering the rather singular circumstance that it was not in connection with an overdue account. The business over, he said he believed I was a writer, and if so, would I mind giving him an introduction to Elinor Glyn? He had a high opinion of her stories of passion, and he had an experience of his own which he was certain would interest her, and about which he would like to ask her advice.

I said that I was afraid I did not know Elinor Glyn. He replied that as an author I must be entitled to approach her on his behalf. Looking at him with some attention I perceived that his indeterminate pale face and receding chin were deceptive, and that his eyes and mouth betokened great obstinacy. To switch him off Elinor Glyn, I said that I would be glad to hear his story. He replied that when I had heard it he was sure I would have no objection to approaching Elinor Glyn.

About seven years ago, he said, he was working in a firm side by side with a young woman who, he noticed, was fond of the men, and had a great many admirers. She was one of the free kind. A friendship sprang up between them, and one evening, when the others had left the office, it 'reached the stage of demonstrated affection', as he put it.

Once, I gathered, was quite enough for the girl. But finding that she would have nothing more to do with him, he became frantic about her. 'I used to follow her to her place of business, wherever it was, and she moved about a lot to escape me. I used to walk in on her, and beg her to take me back. I put detectives on her to find out if she was going with other men. Three years ago I married a girl who was as crazy about me as I am about this other one. I did it from a feeling of service, not self, and what I say is, if I have married my wife because she loves me, this woman ought to live with me because I love her. My wife is willing, and I had a deed drawn up by a lawyer, stating that my wife was willing, and that therefore no obstacle existed to debar this woman from giving me what I had given my wife.'

I asked him if he did not consider the woman's reluctance to live with him, as evidenced by her many flights, a sufficient obstacle to their union. 'Service, not self,' he replied. 'I've done it for my wife, and the other ought to do it for me.'

If, he added, I did not want to approach Elinor Glyn myself, perhaps I would be so good as to ascertain her address, and forward a letter from him asking for an appointment. I told him that I had no intention of adding a third victim to the two he was already persecuting, and showed him out rather brusquely. As I was closing the front door, he said: 'If you should care to reconsider the matter, a note to my business address will always find me, but I should be obliged if you will mark it "private", to avert eventualities.'

Doyle and Kipling

Michael having said that he had never read Sherlock Holmes, Pearson brought him back the collected short stories from Hastings on the following day, and glanced through them after Michael had been urged by his uncle not to spoil the effect of his holiday by staying up too late.

Pearson: Doyle has never had justice done to him as a short-story writer. I am not at all sure that he isn't the best short-story writer, technically speaking, in the English language. What I mean is, that he holds the interest throughout, and leaves one with a vivid impression of the actors. The reason he remains the best of all detective fiction writers is that he never forgets that the fiction is more important than the detection.

Kingsmill: He has such extraordinary variety, too. The Brigadier Gerard stories are, I think, even more exciting than the Holmes ones, and certainly more amusing. And then there are the stories about prizefighters and pirates, and the scientific and mystery thrillers, and so on.

Pearson: Some one once said there were only seven plots in the world. That may have been true before Conan Doyle, who proved that there were at least seventy.

Kingsmill: He was really a kind of medium for all the longing for excitement and bloodshed which had accumulated in the nineteenth century. And so, this longing having been satisfied for the time being by the Great War, and life holding no further interest for him, he turned to another plane, and tried to be its medium.

Pearson: And being mediumistic, no one has ever taken him seriously as an interpreter of life.

Kingsmill: Which is just, though it seems unkind. A good example of his essential unreality is the story of the well-to-do and respected English colonial gentleman, Copley Banks, who becomes a pirate in order to trap the infamous Captain Sharkey. Sharkey had murdered Copley Banks's wife and children, and Copley Banks collects a crew of desperadoes, and in order to gain Sharkey's confidence spends two years looting and massacring on the high seas. Then he meets Sharkey, who visits him on board his own ship as a twin spirit. Copley Banks blows Sharkey up, and the last we see of Copley Banks he is walking inland with a singing in his heart. For Conan Doyle, who is only interested in action, the story is over. To any one interested in human nature, the story is just beginning. It is as if *Macbeth* ended with the thane whistling 'Should Auld Acquaintance Be Forgot' as he emerged from Duncan's bedchamber.

Pearson: I suppose it's because Kipling isn't only a medium, but had some individual sense of life, that he was taken seriously as a writer, while Doyle was dismissed as a mere entertainer.

Kingsmill: And in order to justify ranking Kipling above Doyle, people made the fantastic assumption that he wrote better short stories. Not only did he not write better stories than Doyle, he wrote worse stories than any one else.

Pearson: Isn't that a bit strongly put?

Kingsmill: I like that from you! However, perhaps it could be toned down. All the same, Kipling ruins his stories by long-winded pretentious openings, in which he takes the centre of the stage as the man in the know; his characters are as unreal as Doyle's, and nothing like so vivid; and his plots are not worth the trouble it takes to disentangle them. But when he leaves himself out, which he does at least once . . .

Pearson: Twice. . . .

Kingsmill: He writes, of course, with far more reality than Doyle. *Without Benefit of Clergy*, for example.

Pearson: And *The Man Who Would Be King.*

Kingsmill: But as literature consists almost exclusively of greater writers than Kipling, if I had to choose between him and Conan Doyle I would keep the man who succeeded in telling exciting stories in preference to the man who failed to tell good ones.

Pearson on Buses

On August 19th, two days before Kingsmill left Whatlington, the friends took a bus for Hastings. Kingsmill had already been there a few times for a bathe; he had become accustomed to the barbed wire on the front, and was not altogether sure that he did not prefer it to the August crowds; the place no longer seemed unreal and melancholy to him; and he was anxious to show Pearson one of the finest views in England, from St. Helen's Cemetery. Pearson consenting, they mounted a bus at the Memorial and set off.

Kingsmill: It's a rise of nearly five hundred feet.

Pearson: In Persia, when I wanted to reach a level of five hundred feet, I had to descend into Mesopotamia.

Kingsmill: Any tobacco on you?

Pearson: Yes.

Kingsmill: Edgeworth?

Pearson: Good God, no! I've almost forgotten what it tastes like. My pouch at the moment contains bits of about sixteen brands, I should say. Oh, for the fragrant scent of good old Edgeworth again! Some people, by the way, think it too fragrant. My sister says she can always tell I've been in her house some forty-eight hours after I've left it. And once, on the top of a bus—not, like this, an open top—a man was rude enough to complain of it. However, I showed restraint.

Kingsmill: After not showing it?

Pearson: You can judge that for yourself. The man leant over from the seat immediately behind me, and said in a very pointed manner: 'That's a pungent tobacco you are smoking, sir?'

'Are you a commercial traveller?' I asked.

'No. Why?'

'I thought you might be trying to sell me a rival brand.'

'No, sir.'

'My mistake. But, you see, my tobacco has to be strong, especially on buses. I use it as a disinfectant.'

After pondering this for a while, he said: 'May I ask if that is meant for an insult?'

'You may. It is.'

He sat back, murmuring something I failed to catch, and then moved to another seat.

Kingsmill: Did you feel any desire to look round, to see if he had recovered his peace of mind?

Pearson: He had been rude to me, and I retorted in kind. That is my practice, and I never feel any compunction.

Kingsmill: Do you remember that stout chap who fared rather better with you when you crossed swords on a bus?

Pearson: Very vaguely. In fact, very very vaguely. But, as a friend of mine, you have doubtless retained the episode in all its details.

Kingsmill: He was taking up much more than his fair share of the seat, and having waited for him to move up, you said:

'Perfectly comfortable, are you?'

'Perfectly,' he replied.

'Meaning that you don't intend to move up?'

'You can sit on my knee, if you like.'

'I'm damned if I will!'

'Nobody asked you to.'

Pearson thanked his friend for recalling the incident. The bus had now reached the cemetery, and they went in.

St. Paul

As a biographer, Kingsmill said, Pearson would find the cemetery as uninspiring as any other—all light, or at any rate no shade, in the epitaphs. '*At Rest* predominates,' he said. 'Non-committal and inexpensive. I have sometimes tried to think out something with less than six letters. *Dead* is too obvious, and if the Latinist among the survivors suggested *Vale*, the others would say it didn't make any sense without *Of Tears*, and not much with it.'

Pearson said that the most perfect epitaph he had ever heard was spoken by a farmer in the next compartment while the train was standing in Leominster station one day towards the end of October, 1939: 'There was an old lady who died here three weeks ago, an' she was an hundred, an' she had eleven children, an' her name was Mrs. Firkin.'

'This beats even the view from Tomnahurich Cemetery,' said Pearson, as the weald came into sight beyond a low uneven wall which bounded the cemetery to the north. After looking over the weald for some minutes, they walked to the eastern end of the cemetery, and another superb view lay before them—Romney Marsh and Rye and Winchelsea, and, as they turned, the whole line of the coast to Beachy Head, as far to the west as Dungeness to the east.

Rye, Pearson said, as they left the cemetery, was now associated for him with St. Paul. 'I went there on the thirtieth of last May, and entered the church. The Bible being open on the lectern, I read the last chapter of the Epistle to the Galatians. Previously I had disliked him, having had too much of him in church as a boy. I also had a vague feeling that he was anti-Christian, in the sense that Christ was antipathetic to him; and whatever I may think of Christians, that doesn't spoil the story in the Gospels.

'I hadn't looked at St. Paul since I was at school, and this chapter bowled me completely over. It contains the whole spirit of religion, and therefore disposes of all forms and ceremonies and institutions.

'No wonder St. Paul couldn't stomach St. Peter, the patron saint of the Catholic Church. I have no doubt that when he said one must suffer fools gladly, he had St. Peter in mind, and I have equally no doubt that this was an afterthought, from which Peter himself derived no benefit.'

Kingsmill: All the same, Peter is very lovable, and if left to himself would have made a hash of founding a Village Institute.

This and That

They went down, past St. Helen's Wood, to Old Roar, and as they stood on the bridge over the ravine Kingsmill recalled that it was already nearly five years since they had walked up there and Pearson had suggested the tour round Scotland in the steps of Johnson and Boswell.

'How fantastic it seems!' Pearson exclaimed. 'This isn't the way to make money.'

'Or to grow younger,' Kingsmill murmured.

They went on down to Alexandra Park, which since Kingsmill had left Hastings had been immensely improved in its upper half by the removal of the railings, but damaged further on by the substitution of onions for dahlias in the flower beds. It was preposterous, Pearson cried, that the small space given to the common man should be made repulsive with onions, when thousands of acres all over the country belonging to the rich were lying fallow. Kingsmill surmised that the Town Council, having been compelled to beautify the upper portion of the park by removing the railings, needed a litter of leeks to calm their jangled nerves.

Before taking the bus for Whatlington, they went into a pub near the Memorial. Warmed by two double whiskies, they mounted the bus, and from the top deck

Pearson, looking down on Wellington Square, observed a man reassuring his wife and children, who had been alarmed by a passing aeroplane. 'Probably,' he said, 'some harmless German paterfamilias is doing the same thing at this very moment in Cologne. We're all in the same boat really. Why get savage with any one? We're all children of God. This may be the effect of a couple of double whiskies, but in any case *in vino veritas*.'

France

As the bus went along the front, with a view of the evening sea and a suggestion of the coast of France beyond, Pearson said: 'Whenever I step on to the soil of France, a great load of care and worry seems to lift from me. The world is re-born, and one sees men and women afresh, every one running about on the quaysides, every one chattering and laughing with every one else, a general joyful jumble, little cafés straggling over the pavements, and a donkey trotting down a crowded street and pausing to browse over the bonnet of a motor car, while an express train threads its way between the pedestrians at four or five miles an hour.'

'And I feel sure we'll see all that once more,' said Kingsmill. 'The French will rise again; but if we do that book on France we've talked about, we must be very careful to postpone our arrival until they have finished rising. We don't want to feature in the recovery of their self-respect. It would be a great mistake to provoke a cry of "*sacrés Anglais*", and find ourselves panting through the streets of Caen in our pyjamas, a mob of Madame Defarges, with flying udders, on our heels—cobbles and gables and crumbling arches and glimpses of historic piles and whiffs of historic drainage forming the whole of which we had dreamed, and receiving our last strangled malediction as the process of dismemberment sets in."

Dying for Beethoven

After supper Kingsmill, lamenting that Pearson had not brought his gramophone from London, said he was dying for some Beethoven.

Pearson: That was Bakunin's intention, too.

Kingsmill: ?

Pearson: I have just been reading E. H. Carr's *Life of Bakunin*. On April 1st, 1849, Richard Wagner conducted Beethoven's Ninth Symphony at the

Dresden Opera House, and afterwards Bakunin went up to congratulate him, saying that if all the music that had ever been written should perish in the world conflagration, they must pledge themselves to rescue this symphony, even at the peril of their lives. At that moment Bakunin was planning a world revolution, and a few weeks after his remark to Wagner an insurrection broke out in Dresden. Bakunin, of course, was with the insurgents, who promptly set fire to the Opera House. Wagner fled to Switzerland, and the Ninth Symphony was left to look after itself. In those pre-gramophone days the destruction of a big opera house killed Beethoven for a large number of people. So much for Bakunin's willingness to die for Beethoven.

Kingsmill: Would you have thrown your body between the insurgents and the continued potentiality of playing the Ninth Symphony to the Dresdeners?

Pearson: I certainly wouldn't. But then I wouldn't have pretended I was ready to. I think the Ninth Symphony is worth living for. If I were dead I couldn't enjoy it. The only things really worth dying for are the only things really worth living for.

Kingsmill: You mean, one can't testify to Falstaff at the stake? It would clash with the Master's teaching?

Pearson: Exactly.

Kingsmill: One way, of course, in which people could martyr themselves for art would be to leave all their money to necessitous artists, and then die.

But, at the moment, Raisley Calvert is the only example I can recall of that particular form of martyrdom, and the fact that, after he had willed all his money to Wordsworth, the poet remained with him night and day till the end, leaves it rather doubtful how much free will he exercised in the matter.

Pearson: And while Wordsworth was taking his gruel to the dying Raisley, Beethoven was compelled to sell his Mass to four different publishers, in order to make an honest living.

Kingsmill: Your dates are a little . . .

Pearson: The only decent act ever performed by a corporate body was when the London Philharmonic Society sent Beethoven a hundred pounds. It was a recognition of the fact that Beethoven ought to have been an Englishman. We lead the world in everything but music. We have the greatest literature, the loveliest scenery, the most delightful landscape painters, the most varied and pleasant climate and the most inspiring architecture in the world. But for beer and music we must go to

Germany. Once we had the best beer and the best music, too. Now . . . !

Kingsmill: Elgar?

Pearson: Elgar was the swallow that didn't make a summer. He is in the running with Bach, Mozart, Schubert and the rest, but the merits of these are disputable. The transcendent merit of Beethoven

is indisputable: his music alone constitutes a whole summer of creation. The man who cannot perceive that he outshines all other composers is like the man who cannot perceive that Shakespeare outshines all other writers.

Literature, Music and Painting

Kingsmill: I have always found it impossible to decide whether a supremely great painter or musician or poet lacks anything through not being all three. Is there anything in Rembrandt which Shakespeare or Beethoven doesn't give in his medium, or in them which is missing in Rembrandt? I have never been able to get a musician or a painter to throw any light on this question, or indeed on any other. Possibly they could whistle or sketch an answer, but so far they haven't obliged.

Pearson: My own feeling is that Shakespeare gives you nearly everything that Beethoven or Rembrandt is capable of, and a great deal over. Shallow is more complex and more vivid than any portrait of Rembrandt's; I get a more overwhelming sense of storm in Henry IV's 'wet sea-boy' speech than in

the Sixth Symphony; I feel the tragedy of life more strongly in *Lear* than in the slow movement of the Ninth; for comedy neither music nor painting is capable of conveying anything in the same hemisphere with Falstaff; and for beauty there are lines scattered all over Shakespeare's plays that move me quite as much as any passage in Beethoven. Well, what have you to say?

Kingsmill: So I'm left to hold this prodigious three-headed infant? As I'm neither a painter nor a musician, I always feel a desire to transfer into words the emotion music and painting stir in me, whereas Shakespeare, Goethe or Wordsworth seem complete to me at their best. So I suppose poetry satisfies me more than the other two, but on the other hand I have never found in poetry the exact equivalents of some paintings by Rembrandt and Constable, and some music of Beethoven and Mozart.

Pearson: I grant that there is nothing in poetry like the Last Quartets of Beethoven.

Kingsmill: Which is perhaps not the fault of poetry, but of poets. If Shakespeare had gone on from *Lear*, instead of collapsing, *The Tempest* would have been his Last Quartets. There is a hint of what he might have written in Caliban's 'Be not afeard. . . .'

The Coloured Counties

After some weeks with his family at Hinton-St.-George, Kingsmill returned to Woods Place for another spell of work before term started. Wandering one evening in the neighbouring fields, he and Pearson were struck afresh by the different colours in the landscape and by the different tints of green, all seeming to blend to a perfect whole. 'Colours which obviously clash when placed in conjunction by artifice are always harmonious in nature,' observed Pearson. 'Colours don't clash in nature,' said Kingsmill, 'because any combination of colours in nature strikes us as natural.' 'Naturally,' said Pearson. They agreed that the country had been vastly improved by the advent of the motor car. They could remember how dusty the hedgerows used to be in August when they were young, before the coming of the tarmac road. Now all was unspoilt and green.

Kingsmill wanted to know whether Pearson could define the difference between Somerset and Sussex. 'Somerset,' he said, while Pearson was gathering his ideas, 'seems older, deeper and more secret—whatever that means, and it does mean something. I believe I am right in saying, and if any member of the Lower Fourth were here he would probably support me, that in pre-historic times that part of England was inhabited by tribes which did not get so far as here. But not to go back to cavemen, even the trees down there seem older. There are oaks in the park at Hinton-St.-George which are, from their look, well over a thousand years of age. They would be an eye-opener to that surveyor we met in Savernake. But on the whole I prefer this country. It is lighter, more aerial, less soaked in the pains and struggles of humanity. No place in the world is so lovely as this part of Sussex.'

Pearson: Except the other part of Sussex. I admit that the weald hereabouts is prettier than the weald north of Arundel. But the Downs that stretch east and west of Arundel, the little wooded hollows in them, the tree-crowned chalkpits, the tufted rings, the friendly contours of the soft bare hills, have no parallel on earth.

'Here through the long unhampered days
    The tinkling silence thrills;
And little, lost, Down churches praise
    The Lord who made the hills.'

Kingsmill: You have substituted 'long' for 'strong' in

the first line; poetry for Kipling. It is as big an improvement as the Autolycus verse. Hadn't you better take in hand the whole corpus of English poetry?

Pearson: My improvements are instinctive, but if I sat down to the job the intention would wreck the inspiration. I remember an occasion when Colin Hurry and I made a perfect transposition in Gray's Eton ode. We were in Persia; and looking at some children playing in the dirt at Kermanshah I began to recite:

> 'Alas! regardless of their doom
>   The little victims play;
> No sense have they of ills to come
>   Nor care beyond to-day. . . .'

By this time Colin was chanting the poem with me, and without any hesitation we went straight on:

> 'Yet ah! why should they know their fate,
> Since sorrow never comes too late,
> And happiness too swiftly flies?
> Thought would destroy their paradise.
> No more: where ignorance is bliss
>   'Tis folly to be wise.'

Kingsmill: Is paradise destroyed by thought? If so, England should be a happy place. But to return to Sussex, have you nothing to say on behalf of Worcestershire?

Pearson: I suppose one's native county has a special

attraction. According to Belloc, we in Worcestershire have 'the secret of the rocks, and the oldest
kind of song'. We also have the Severn with its
wonderful high banks and exquisite tributaries,
the Malvern Hills with their noble outline, and
Elgar with his Slow Movements.

Kingsmill: I was born by the Thames—46 Torrington
Square, to be precise. I wish my first impressions
of the English country had been in Worcestershire,
but they were in the Lincolnshire Wolds, and there
is something gloomy about all the eastern counties.
It was from Lincolnshire to Cambridge that
Cromwell collected his army. Flat country seems
to produce puritans. In lowland men of genius,
Constable and Rembrandt, beauty is created in
revulsion against the surrounding flatness. In
ordinary men the country breeds an image of
itself.

Pearson: The Midlands are perhaps even less inspiring
than the eastern counties, though I must put in a
word for the river Ouse, on the banks of which
I spent so many holidays as a youngster and which
has spoilt bathing for me in any other river, to
say nothing of the sea. Also Bedfordshire villages
are far prettier than Devonshire ones. It seems
that in dull country people are forced in self-
defence to improve the landscape with lovely
villages and towns, whereas in beautiful country
they leave beautiful effects to nature.

Kingsmill: And I must put in a word for the river
Trent at Burton, with its wide soothing curves,
by which one imagines fat abbots jogging along on
their palfreys. And in any case I would rather

be settled either in the Midlands or the eastern counties than in the steamy lushness of Devonshire, which was just the county to produce a shapeless creature like Coleridge, who, like Devonshire, enchants at first and cloys in the end.

Pearson: Whereas the Lakes produced the rocklike Wordsworth. . . .

Kingsmill: . . . fresh, tranquil and sublime.

Pearson: Bucks and Herts are so lovely in some places that one can forget they are Metroland in others. But I at any rate must award the palm to the counties through which the river Severn runs—Worcestershire, Gloucestershire and Shropshire. These are the heart and soul of England.

Kingsmill: I think they are too near Wales for that. Something Celtic breathes over them from the Welsh hills. The heart of England is elusive. I remember a Notts man telling me that you can find it in Nottinghamshire. The men of Notts, he said, were of predominantly Danish stock, but nearer the sea there was always some admixture of foreign blood—Flemings in Suffolk, Frenchmen in Sussex, Spaniards, if I recollect aright, in Dorsetshire, and Carthaginians in Cornwall. Perhaps each individual should be left to decide this question for himself. To some the heart of a country will be where they have felt most, whether pain or happiness, or both. To others it will be some place which they hardly know, but in which they believe they would have found something they have missed elsewhere. Wordsworth represents the first type, Housman the second.

This Blessed Plot

On their last Sunday, September 14th, Pearson took Kingsmill on his favourite walk in the neighbourhood of Whatlington. It ran through Vinehall Park, about half-way across which a tree-trunk at the edge of a spinney made a seat on which Pearson had frequently meditated, pacified by a pipe and tranquillized by as lovely a view as England affords.

Going across the fields between Woods Place and the main Hastings-London road, Kingsmill pointed to an exquisite little valley beneath them and asked why Pearson had not shown it to him before. 'We have traversed these meadows at least six times since you have been here,' said Pearson, 'and it is no fault of mine that you have done so with your eyes shut. However, I am forced to admit that every time I pass this spot I seem to see that valley afresh. The English countryside at its best is a perpetual revelation.' They came out into the main road, walked along it until Mountfield Halt was behind them, then turned right just beyond the disused gate of the lodge, 'hented' three stiles-a, and slowly ascended the hill on the top of which stands Vinehall House, now occupied by soldiers. They seated themselves on the trunk, and Pearson, not altogether suppressing an air of being responsible for the scene before them, remained silent while his friend took it in. Beyond the dingle which ran along the foot of the hill, a hundred yards or more from where they were sitting, the ground rose slowly, and in the motionless rain-laden atmosphere they could smell the bracken on the far slope. To their right a new but harmonious house showed through trees, and on the near side of the trees the rich brown of two ploughed fields heightened the surrounding green. In the distance they saw the windmill by Battle, and ridges of low wooded hills undulating towards the hidden sea.

'When I was young,' said Pearson, 'I used to run down England, the reason being that my country stood for all I then knew about life—school discipline, parental authority, the established religion, and everything else against which I was in healthy revolt. Though a Tory in politics, because I had been brought up to believe that it was bad taste to be anything else, I was a natural rebel, and England to me was simply the home of what I most disliked and kicked against. Yet here am I, sitting on this log in my fifties, brimming over with sentiment for England, and convinced, after knocking and being knocked about the universe at intervals for over thirty years, that ours is the only delectable country and its inhabitants the only decent people on earth. How can I explain it?'

> *Kingsmill:* In youth one expects other countries to be better than one's own, just as one expects new acquaintances to be of quite a different and superior stamp to old ones. Later one is drawn back to the people and the language through which one has felt life most deeply, unless of course one has come to hate life so much that one's own country focuses this hatred most strongly just because it is the country one knows best. That is why treachery in war-time is so horrifying. Not because it is equivalent to a vote of no confidence in the government, or an expression of dissatisfaction

with the prevailing social system, but because of the abyss of self-loathing it reveals. To work for the enemy, or even to hope for his victory, is to confess complete spiritual bankruptcy. Treachery may disguise itself as a reasonable wish for power, refused by one's own countrymen and now bestowed by a more far-sighted government. But essentially it is a denial that life has anything to offer beyond the gratification of egotism, that neither the earthly affections nor the spiritual intuitions which are interwoven with one's own land have any value.

Pearson: True enough. But in considering patriotism as an abstraction, you have wandered from the point I was making—namely, my profound conviction that the English are the best of all peoples. Why do I consider them the best? The explanation seems to be that, lacking any fanatical element in myself, I love a nation that does not go off the deep end on the slightest provocation. We are a balanced race. Our main virtue is that we never feel enthusiasm for abstract ideals. Humour is our greatest gift, our divinely rational merit. Kings may come and kings may go, but we scarcely trouble to notice whether a Plantagenet is followed by a Tudor, a Tudor by a Stuart, a Stuart by a Dictator, a Dictator by a Stuart, a Stuart by a Dutchman, a Dutchman by a Hanoverian, or even (as we have seen recently) a Hanoverian by a Hanoverian. We change our religions with equal indifference. Neither the agitation of a dispossessed Pope nor the fury of a falling monarch can create enough interest among us to bring a crowd into the streets. We are in fact a nation of individualists, which is all to the good.

Kingsmill: Potentially, we are more individual than other peoples. Actually, we produce one Johnson for ten million more or less indistinguishable persons. Why is the Englishman so tongue-tied? Because he ought to be a poet, but has enough sense to know he isn't one. Englishmen never find their tongues except in public telephone booths, where the person addressed is invisible, or in after-dinner speeches, where the persons addressed are indistinguishable. But for the most part the English keep themselves to themselves, without taking much trouble to make their own company worth while.

Pearson: I agree that our habit of not caring a tinker's curse for anything outside ourselves needs to be checked. We have reached a point where we feel that nothing concerns us, and so we have become the most easily exploited of peoples, the most easily duped. Only ten years ago we were scared into cutting a few pence off the miserable pittance doled out to the unemployed, and only two years ago we were paralysed into spending untold billions on a war for which we were wholly unprepared. In fact our politicians are allowed to do, or leave undone, what they like, and what they left undone between 1919 and 1939 would have wrecked us for ever if we had not had the astounding good fortune to run up against the biggest fool even we have ever had to contend with.

Kingsmill: We never have done anything between wars. Hence our energy during them.

Pearson: It is also due to our indifference that the workers of these islands, who ought to be rolling in the illimitable wealth of our Empire, are half-starved, poorly-clad, disgracefully housed, and scandalously unreceptive to everything that makes life worth living: great literature, great music, great architecture, and the miraculous loveliness of the English countryside.

Our rich rush about the earth trying to distract themselves from themselves; our poor content themselves with betting on dogs and filling in football coupons. And who can blame them? They are always in need of money; it gives their starved souls a thrill; and the recreations of the rich are just as futile. Here we touch the root of the trouble. Because of their intense individualism the British respect wealth and titles, which denote individual success. Unlike the French, they do not merely want riches themselves: they actually admire rich people: which means that they also admire what rich people do, and to the best of their ability copy them.

Kingsmill: It is all part of their undeveloped poetry. A Frenchman wants to enjoy the pleasures within his reach; an Englishman, in his sheepish way, aspires towards what he conceives to be the ideal life of the rich.

Pearson: In other words our undeveloped poetry is rapidly turning us into a stupid bestial nation. 'What is a man,' says Hamlet, 'if his chief good and market of his time be but to sleep and feed? A beast; no more.' From the throne downwards we think more of a man who can cheat others in the City, or whose ancestors were gangsters, or who can smack a ball about a field with dexterity, than of a man who can create beauty, or add to the gaiety of life, or deepen its spiritual significance. Queen Elizabeth and her Stuart successors did at least appreciate Shakespeare, and the nobles of those days patronized the poets. Recent monarchs prefer Cup Finals, and modern nobles are patronized by film stars. We are not even sufficiently aware of our shame to give lip-service to the arts, and our Civil List pensions are a national sin against the Holy Ghost.

Kingsmill: I doubt if it has been easy to be an artist in any age or country. Our monarchs nowadays go to football finals because we are a democracy, and the tastes of the democracy have to be flattered. But the royal approval of Elizabeth and Louis XIV does not seem to have sweetened the lives of Shakespeare and Molière.

Life is difficult everywhere and for every one, but I would rather have lived it as an Englishman of this time than in any other age or country.

Pearson: You will tell me next that our modern domestic architecture is as good as can reasonably be expected, and another sign of our undeveloped poetry. Blind, deaf and dumb though they are to the arts, the English people have got to live somewhere, and so we see in their domestic architecture the outward and visible sign of their inward and spiritual disgrace. Houses of a dozen different styles—our individualism at its vilest—jostling one another in the same terrace. Beauty, comfort, utility, health, all sacrificed to the desire of the rich man to erect something as cheap as possible in order to make a lot, and the desire of the poor man to pay as little as possible in order to save a bit. The foulness of our domestic architecture began with the industrial revolution, and has been steadily growing fouler. Think of the charm of Tudor houses and the beauty of Jacobean, the dignity of the Anne period and the spaciousness of the Georgian; and then think, if you can bear to, of the vulgar blatancy of Victorian buildings and the shoddy shacks of to-day.

Kingsmill: It was just because industrialism made English life so hideous that the—pardon me !—un-developed poetry in our nature has sprouted in all these imitations of Spanish, French and Italian palaces, chateaux, and so on, with their romantic names, Avalon, Mio Sogno, Samarcand, and the rest. But have you no word of cheer about the only delectable country and the only decent people on earth?

Pearson: We have not yet lost our one great virtue, humour, which saves us from utter damnation and enables us to retain our individualities, such as they are. Falstaff would have approved the lads of the Merchant Navy whose ship was torpedoed the other day, and who cruised about for some time in their lifeboat. Suddenly they spotted a submarine, which they thought was the boat which had sunk them returning to sink them again. But an English voice yelled out: 'Do you want a lift?', and they yelled back: 'Yes, put us off at Piccadilly Circus.'

A minute or two passed in silence. Pearson, whose

anger 'shows a hasty spark, and straight is cold again', gazed at the landscape with mild benevolence.

'It must have been in some such peaceful spot as this,' said Kingsmill dreamily, 'nothing more dangerous within ten miles of him than a fieldmouse, that it occurred to Shakespeare that come the three corners of the world in arms, and we shall shock them: Nought shall make us rue, if England to itself do rest but true.'

Printed in Great Britain by
Wyman & Sons, Ltd., London, Fakenham and Reading.